Jams, Pickles & Chutneys

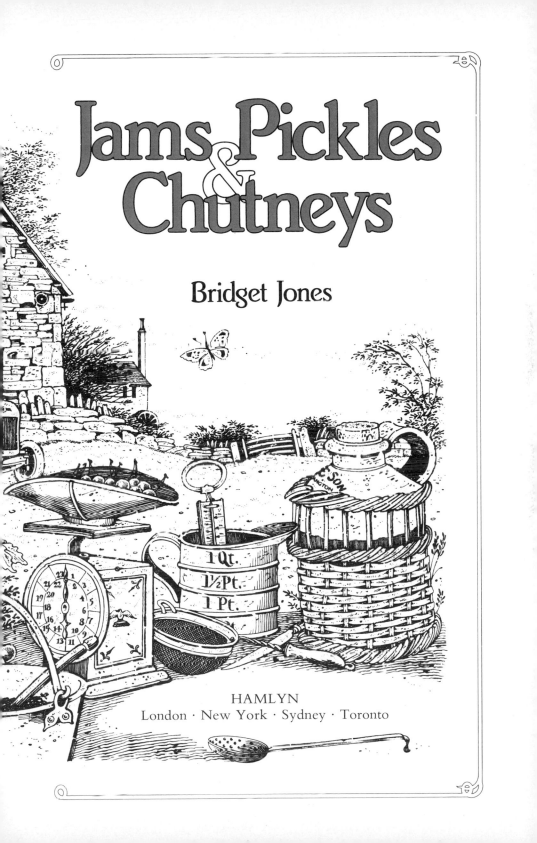

Jams Pickles & Chutneys

Bridget Jones

HAMLYN
London · New York · Sydney · Toronto

To Neill – and Pickles the cat

The following titles are also available in this series:
Barbecue Cookbook · Contact Grill
Chicken Cookbook · Cocktails and Mixed Drinks
Cooking for One, Two or More · The Diabetic Cookbook
Egg and Cheese Cookbook · Fred's Pastry Cookbook
Hamlyn Curry Cookbook · Hamlyn Pressure Cookbook
Kitchen Magic · Mighty Mince Cookbook

The publishers would like to thank Elizabeth David Limited and the
General Trading Company Limited
for supplying products for use in the photographs.

Cover photographs by Martin Brigdale
Photography by Martin Brigdale

Line illustrations by Anthony Sidwell

First published in 1983 by
The Hamlyn Publishing Group Limited
London · New York · Sydney · Toronto
Astronaut House, Feltham, Middlesex, England
© Copyright The Hamlyn Publishing Group Limited 1983

ISBN 0 600 32326 9

Set in 11 on 12pt Bembo 270
by Photocomp Limited, Birmingham, England

Printed in Italy

Contents

Useful Facts and Figures

Notes on metrication

In this book quantities are given in metric and Imperial measures. Exact conversion from Imperial to metric measures does not usually give very convenient working quantities and so the metric measures have been rounded off into units of 25 grams. The table below shows the recommended equivalents.

Ounces	Approx g to nearest whole figure	Recommended conversion to nearest unit of 25	Ounces	Approx g to nearest whole figure	Recommended conversion to nearest unit of 25
1	28	25	11	312	300
2	57	50	12	340	350
3	85	75	13	368	375
4	113	100	14	396	400
5	142	150	15	425	425
6	170	175	16 (1 lb)	454	450
7	198	200	17	482	475
8	227	225	18	510	500
9	255	250	19	539	550
10	283	275	20 ($1\frac{1}{4}$ lb)	567	575

Note When converting quantities over 20 oz first add the appropriate figures in the centre column, then adjust to the nearest unit of 25. As a general guide, 1 kg (1000 g) equals 2·2 lb or about 2 lb 3 oz. This method of conversion gives good results in nearly all cases, although in certain pastry and cake recipes a more accurate conversion is necessary to produce a balanced recipe.

Liquid measures The millilitre has been used in this book and the following table gives a few examples.

Imperial	Approx ml to nearest whole figure	Recommended ml	Imperial	Approx ml to nearest whole figure	Recommended ml
$\frac{1}{4}$ pint	142	150 ml	1 pint	567	600 ml
$\frac{1}{2}$ pint	283	300 ml	$1\frac{1}{2}$ pints	851	900 ml
$\frac{3}{4}$ pint	425	450 ml	$1\frac{3}{4}$ pints	992	1000 ml (1 litre)

Spoon measures All spoon measures given in this book are level unless otherwise stated.
Can sizes At present, cans are marked with the exact (usually to the nearest whole number) metric equivalent of the Imperial weight of the contents, so we have followed this practice when giving can sizes.

Notes for American and Australian users

In America the 8-oz measuring cup is used. In Australia metric measures are now used in conjunction with the standard 250-ml measuring cup. The Imperial pint, used in Britain and Australia, is 20 fl oz, while the American pint is 16 fl oz. It is important to remember that the Australian tablespoon differs from both the British and American tablespoons; the table below gives a comparison. The British standard tablespoon, which has been used throughout this book, holds 17.7 ml, the American 14.2 ml, and the Australian 20 ml. A teaspoon holds approximately 5 ml in all three countries.

British	American	Australian	British	American	Australian
1 teaspoon	1 teaspoon	1 teaspoon	$3\frac{1}{2}$ tablespoons	4 tablespoons	3 tablespoons
1 tablespoon	1 tablespoon	1 tablespoon	4 tablespoons	5 tablespoons	$3\frac{1}{2}$ tablespoons
2 tablespoons	3 tablespoons	2 tablespoons			

An Imperial/American guide to liquid measures

Imperial	American	Imperial	American
$\frac{1}{4}$ pint liquid	$\frac{2}{3}$ cup liquid	1 pint	$2\frac{1}{2}$ cups
$\frac{1}{2}$ pint	$1\frac{1}{4}$ cups	$1\frac{1}{2}$ pints	$3\frac{3}{4}$ cups
$\frac{3}{4}$ pint	2 cups	2 pints	5 cups ($2\frac{1}{2}$ pints)

Note: When making any of the recipes in this book, only follow one set of measures as they are not interchangeable.

Foreword

FROM THE many hours that we all spend cooking our day-to-day meals, there can be few that yield as satisfying results as those invested in making preserves. When the hot jam is poured into the pots, the waxed discs pressed on and the labels neatly written, you will feel a glowing pride and immense sense of achievement. I use the word 'invested' because when you are preparing these preserves you are investing in the flavour of fresh foods for later use.

To show you that there is nothing particularly difficult about home preserving, I have tried to make the recipes as simple as possible, but at the same time I have used combinations of unusual ingredients and warming spices which will, I hope, inspire you to try some unfamiliar recipes as well as the very basic ones. Where expensive or less abundant ingredients are used they are combined with simple fruits or vegetables which emphasise the flavour while adding bulk. In addition you will find a note at the top of each recipe which offers some guidance as to what you can expect from the results as well as a few ideas for serving.

I hope you will feel as much satisfaction in making these preserves as I do and as my husband, Neill, does in devouring them!

Bridget Jones

Introduction

THE PRESERVATION of the foods of summer is no longer a necessity for our survival in the winter months. Time-tested techniques of drying and salting have, to a large extent, been replaced by advances in bottling, canning and most recently by the advent of home freezing. The success, economy and ease of modern freezing has put this method to the fore of the home-preserving scene. Even so, traditional favourites such as jams, chutneys and pickles are annually prepared when our home-grown produce is at its best. Excellent local markets, farm shops and pick-your-own fruit farms give everyone the chance to prepare the store cupboard delicacies which will cheer up many a winter teatime spread or cold-roast supper.

Home preserving need not be complicated and the recipes in this book are tested and written for simplicity and success. Divided into five chapters, they cover the basic traditional methods of making jams and jellies; fruit butters and conserves; marmalades and mincemeats; chutneys and ketchups; and pickles and relishes. There is no need to spend a great deal of money on special preserving equipment before you try the recipes, as most kitchens are adequately equipped for jam and chutney preparation and the quantities given in the recipes are quite moderate.

The basic utensils that you will need include a measuring jug, kitchen scales, a good sharp knife, a long-handled wooden spoon and a large saucepan. Heavy aluminium, stainless steel and good-quality enamel pans are ideal. Iron and zinc cookware should be avoided and, although copper and brass pans are suitable for making jams, these metals react with acid and are therefore unsuitable for making chutneys and pickles. Remember that jams, jellies and marmalades need to boil rapidly, so make sure that the pan is deep enough to allow for this. A wide-topped preserving pan allows plenty of room for the evaporation of excess moisture, but for many long-cooked chutneys and pickles your pan will need a reasonably well-fitting lid.

For those of you who have a particularly well-equipped kitchen, remember that a food processor or an electric shredder and slicer will cut down the preparation time for most vegetables and some fruit. A pressure cooker is also a great time saver for long-cooked preserves, but always follow the manufacturer's instructions as a guide for timing.

A sugar thermometer provides the easiest and most accurate way of testing for setting. These vary in type and price: the most basic gives only a Fahrenheit scale while the more expensive ones give a Centigrade reading as well, and many have clips which will attach to the side of the pan. Take your pick, but remember that the most basic is probably good enough if you only plan to launch into making sweet preserves on, at the most, a bi-annual basis.

Jellies have to be strained through a jelly bag or a large, clean tea towel and for some jams or marmalades a length of muslin may be required in which to tie up and boil the trimmings. Some jams and fruit butters have to be pressed through a fine sieve and this should preferably be made of nylon.

When the preserve is ready for potting you will find that a small heatproof jug with a good spout is best for pouring. Special wide-necked funnels are available for filling pots but they are not essential. Save all your empty jars, wash them thoroughly and rinse them in plenty of boiling water before use. Jars with airtight lids are essential for chutneys and some pickles but jams, marmalades and sweet preserves may simply be covered with waxed discs applied directly to the surface of the preserve to exclude all air, and the jars topped with pieces of cellophane secured with elastic bands.

When your preserve is finished and ready for storing away, label the pots neatly, stating the name of the preserve, the date on which is was made and, if you have room, a guide as to whether it is a sweet or tart chutney or pickle. With a little imagination, decorative labels and pretty outer material covers will turn a simple pot of preserve into a welcome gift.

Jams and Jellies

HOME-MADE jams bear little or no resemblance to their commercially prepared cousins as they are usually far better flavoured. Right at the beginning of this chapter you will find a chart for making simple fruit jams; this is followed by a detailed guide to the preparation of jams and jellies. The recipes combine fruits which are complementary in flavour and there are a few which make use of the more unusual imported fruits which we find in many of our supermarkets and greengrocers.

Why not try making a jelly for a change? Jellies are always useful for serving with very thin bread and butter or with cold creamy desserts and are often more pleasant to eat than jams made from fruits with lots of pips.

When you have made your jam, set aside a Sunday afternoon, invite a guest to tea and revel in the simple luxury of warm scones, full-flavoured jam and lashings of clotted cream – what a treat!

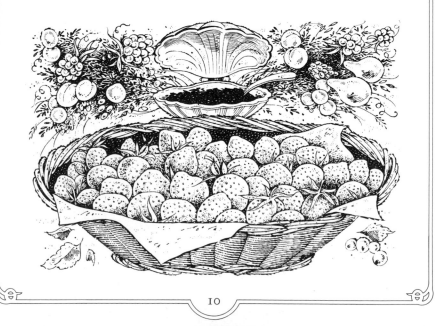

Basic Guide to Making Jams and Jellies

Fruit	Water per 450 g/1 lb	Sugar per 450 g/1 lb	Pectin/Acid
Apple	300 ml/½ pint	350 g/12 oz	juice of 1 lemon
Apricot	150 ml/¼ pint	450 g/1 lb	juice of ½ lemon
Blackberry	2 tablespoons	450 g/1 lb	juice of 1 lemon
Blackcurrant	300 ml/½ pint	575 g/1¼ lb	—
Damson	150 ml/¼ pint	450 g/1 lb	juice of 1 lemon
Gooseeberry	300 ml/½ pint	450 g/1 lb	juice of ½ lemon
Greengage	4 tablespoons	450 g/1 lb	—
Loganberry	1–2 tablespoons	450 g/1 lb	—
Plum	2–4 tablespoons	450 g/1 lb	juice of ½ lemon
Quince	450 ml/¾ pint	575 g/1¼ lb	juice of 1 lemon
Raspberry	1–2 tablespoons	450 g/1 lb	—
Rhubarb	2–4 tablespoons	450 g/1 lb	apple pulp
Strawberry	2 tablespoons	350 g/12 oz	juice of 1 lemon *or* apple pulp

Apple pulp Rinse and roughly chop 450 g/1 lb cooking apples. Place them in a saucepan with 300 ml/½ pint water, bring to the boil, then cook, covered, for 20–25 minutes, until they are reduced to a pulp. Press this pulp through a fine sieve; the resulting purée will give 1.5 kg/3 lb fruit a good set.

Preparing the fruit For best results choose fruit that is not quite ripe, as it will contain the most pectin, without which the jam will not set. Fruit which is just ripe gives the best flavour and should still contain enough pectin, but over-ripe fruit should not be used as it does not make a good jam or jelly. Prepare the fruit according to its type, discarding any that is badly damaged or mouldy. Remove the peel, cores, stones, pips and stalks when making jam, but do not discard any of these trimmings – they often contain a valuable quantity of pectin and may also help to flavour the jam. Instead, add just enough water to cover the trimmings, then boil them for 30 minutes in a covered pan. Uncover the pan and continue cooking until most of the water has evaporated, then press the resulting pulp through a fine sieve. Add the extract to the fruit before cooking. Alternatively, if the fruit will need cooking for some time, the trimmings may be tied up in a piece of muslin or fine cotton and cooked with the fruit. After the fruit has cooled, the muslin should be squeezed of all its juices which are then returned to the pan.

Large fruit – for example apples, peaches or pears – should be sliced thickly; medium-sized fruit – such as apricots, dates and large strawberries – can be halved and the smaller fruits should be left whole. Kernels from the cracked stones of apricots and plums can be added to the fruit.

Softening the fruit Choose a pan large enough to allow plenty of room for the fruit pulp to boil without boiling over. A wide-topped pan is best as it will allow excess liquid to evaporate quickly. It is most important that the fruit is cooked until it is soft *before* the bulk of the sugar is added, as the addition of sugar has a hardening effect on most fruit.

Place the fruit in the pan with the water and about a quarter of the sugar (see the chart on page 11). Raspberries, strawberries and rhubarb require only enough water to moisten the pan, while the tougher fruits like apples, blackcurrants and quinces need considerably more. Heat the mixture slowly to boiling point, stirring as little as possible, just enough to prevent the fruit from sticking to the pan, then cover the pan, reduce the heat and simmer until the fruit is soft. This can take anything from 2–3 minutes for soft fruit – strawberries, raspberries, blackberries – to 20–25 minutes for apples, blackcurrants and damsons.

To make jelly, the cooked fruit has to be strained through a jelly bag or a large, clean tea towel. Place a large bowl on the seat of an upturned stool to catch the jelly and tie the four corners of the jelly bag or towel to the four legs, just above the bowl. Alternatively, hang the bag from a coat-hanger over the bowl placed on a shelf or ledge. Do not squeeze the bag at any time during the straining or the jelly will become cloudy. The fruit should be left to strain overnight to obtain the most extract.

Pectin This is the substance present in fruit which makes the jam set when the correct amount of sugar is added and the fruit is boiled. Pectin is released from the fruit as it is cooked. Some fruits have a good pectin content: lemons, cooking apples and crab-apples, blackcurrants and Seville oranges; others, such as plums and raspberries, have a medium pectin content and many fruits contain little pectin – for example, strawberries, rhubarb and pears.

To test for pectin, take a teaspoonful of the unsweetened cooked fruit pulp and drop it into 2 tablespoons of methylated spirits. Shake well, then pour the mixture into another container. If, as you pour, you see that the fruit pulp has formed a few large clots, it contains plenty of pectin; if several small clots are formed only a soft set will result; but if many small clots pour out, the jam will not set and more pectin should be added. Cooked, sieved apple pulp can be stirred into the fruit at the beginning of the softening process, or lemon juice or commercial pectin stock added towards the end of cooking time. (Commercial pectin stock can be bought at most good chemists; follow the instructions on the packet carefully to obtain a good set.)

Acid   Acid helps to release the pectin from the cells of the fruit and is also needed therefore to set the jam. Lemon juice, again, is a good source of this and it should be added to those fruits which do not naturally contain a great deal of acid, such as apricots, blackberries, plums and strawberries.

Sugar   It is not essential to use preserving sugar, which is more expensive than granulated, but it will dissolve more quickly and causes less scum. Add only the amount that the recipe states, as the proper sugar concentration is vital in obtaining a good set. Gradually stir the sugar into the softened fruit and heat slowly until it dissolves completely. Fruit that has a good pectin content requires up to twice its own weight of sugar. If the sugar content of the jam is inadequate, the natural yeast will start working and the stored jam may start to ferment.

Boiling   Once the sugar has dissolved the jam must be brought to a rapid, rolling boil. The rapid boiling must be maintained until setting point is reached – this can be anything from 5–20 minutes depending on the type, quality and water content of the fruit. Stir the jam at this stage as little as possible, as over-stirring mixes the rising scum back into the jam.

Testing for setting   Start testing after 3–5 minutes of boiling. Unless you are using a thermometer, remove the pan from the heat – do not allow the jam to boil while you are testing or you may overcook it.

There are three ways to test for setting – the thermometer test, the saucer test and the flake test. The thermometer test, using a sugar thermometer to record the temperature of the boiling preserve, is the most accurate. Hold the thermometer well in the jam but clear of the bottom of the saucepan. Most jams and jellies set at 104 C/220 F. For a double check follow this up with the saucer test. Place a spoonful of the jam on a cold saucer. In a few minutes the surface of the jam should develop an obvious skin if setting point has been reached. Push the cooling jam with your finger – if it is ready, the surface should form wrinkles like the skin of hot milk.

The least reliable test is the flake test. Drop a little of the jam off a clean wooden spoon – it should form flakes as it runs off the end of the spoon.

Skimming   Scum rises to the surface during cooking and this has to be removed before the preserve is potted. Use a slotted spoon to lift the scum off the surface of the jam, jelly or marmalade. If the preserve is not a clear one (that is, if it is not a jelly or perhaps a fine marmalade), then a little butter may be stirred in to disperse the scum.

Potting, covering and labelling Pots must be thoroughly cleaned in hot, soapy water, rinsed and dried, then heated with boiling water or in a warm oven. Immediately it is ready, the jam or jelly should be poured into the jars. You can use a clean, small, heatproof jug for filling the jars or you may find a wide-necked funnel useful. Fill them up right to the brim and lay a waxed paper disc, waxed side down, over the surface of the jam so as to exclude all air. The pots can either be covered immediately with airtight lids or allowed to cool completely and then covered with lids or pieces of cellophane, secured with elastic bands. Label the jars neatly with the type of jam or jelly and the date on which it was made, then store them in a cool, dark place. All jams and jellies will keep well for 6–9 months.

What Went Wrong?

Everyone has the occasional disaster with home-made jam, but there is no need to despair. If your jam has not set it could be for one of the following reasons:

Insufficient pectin Certain types of over-ripe fruit may have too little pectin. If the preserve is not already over-boiled, add sieved cooked apple pulp (see the chart, page 11) and boil hard, re-testing for setting.

Insufficient acid Acid is needed to release the pectin from the fruit. If the fruit had little acid the pectin may still be trapped. Check the chart on page 11 to make sure you have added enough acid; if not, try adding lemon juice, citric or tartaric acid now and boil hard.

Inadequate boiling You may not have boiled the preserve hard enough or long enough. Patience is needed for this – carry on boiling and testing if you think all the other requirements are there.

Over-boiling This is disastrous. Overcooked jam will not set. You can tell if the jam has been overcooked by reading its temperature – if it is considerably higher than 104 C/220 F then it has cooked too much. If you really are determined to get the preserve to set you can try adding more water and pectin, but it is not usually worth the effort as you may well end up with a jam which has an inferior flavour, colour and appearance. Better to cut your losses and use it as a sweet fruit sauce to serve with ice creams or puddings, to flavour creams and mousses or to add to a trifle. You can even mix runny jam with canned custard and whipped cream and freeze it into a fruity ice cream!

Gingered Rhubarb and Orange Jam

If you are not too keen on ginger it may be omitted – the jam will be just as delicious.

Makes 2.75–3.25 kg/6–7 lb

1.5 kg/3 lb trimmed rhubarb
50 g/2 oz fresh root ginger
pared rind and juice of 2 oranges
2 lemons
1.15 litres/2 pints water
1.75 kg/4 lb sugar
15 g/$\frac{1}{2}$ oz butter

Slice the rhubarb and put two-thirds of it in a large saucepan. Peel and finely chop the ginger, chop the orange rind and squeeze the juice from the lemons. Mix these ingredients with the rhubarb in the pan and add the orange juice and water. Chop the lemon shells and tie them securely in a piece of clean muslin. Put this in the pan and bring the mixture to the boil. Reduce the heat and simmer steadily for about 1 hour. Do not cover the pan – the fruit should be reduced by half at the end of the simmering time.

Allow to cool, then remove the muslin and squeeze out all the juices from it into the pan. Add the remaining rhubarb, return the jam to the boil and simmer it for about 5–10 minutes, until the fruit is soft. Gradually stir in the sugar and continue stirring over a low heat until it has completely dissolved. Bring the jam once more to the boil and boil hard to setting point.

Stir in the butter to disperse any scum and pour the jam into warmed pots. Top each with a disc of waxed paper, waxed side down, and allow to cool completely. Cover with lids or pieces of cellophane when cold.

Blackberry and Apple Jam

Blackberry and apple jam is delicious on hot toast, in jam tarts, or you can pile it lavishly in the base of a custard tart.

Makes about 3.25 kg/7 lb

1 kg/2 lb blackberries
1.75 kg/4 lb sugar
1 kg/2 lb cooking apples
300 ml/½ pint water
juice of 2 large lemons
25 g/1 oz butter

Make sure that the blackberries are not over-ripe; ideally they should be slightly under-ripe. Pick off any stalks and rinse the fruit. Layer the blackberries with the sugar in a large bowl and leave this to stand overnight.

Peel, core and slice the apples. Place all the trimmings in a saucepan and pour in the water. Bring to the boil and boil, uncovered, for about 20 minutes until most of the water has evaporated and the trimmings are pulpy. Press the mixture through a fine sieve into a large saucepan.

Add the apple slices to the pan and pour in the blackberries with all their juice and any undissolved sugar. Heat the mixture gently to simmering point, stirring to dissolve the sugar, and cook the fruit gently for about 10 minutes, until soft. Pour in the lemon juice.

Bring the jam to the boil and boil hard to setting point. Stir in the butter and pour into warmed pots. Cover the top of the jam with waxed discs, then allow to cool. Top the cold jars with lids or cellophane covers and label neatly.

Blackcurrant and Apple Jam

If you have only a few pounds of fruit on your blackcurrant bushes, you can increase the quantity of jam by adding apples without losing the blackcurrant flavour.

Makes about 2.25 kg/5 lb

1 kg/2 lb apples
450 g/1 lb blackcurrants
600 ml/1 pint water
juice of 2 large lemons
1.5 kg/3 lb sugar
25 g/1 oz butter

Peel, core and slice the apples. Tie the trimmings up in a piece of muslin and place them in a saucepan with the sliced apple, blackcurrants and water. Bring to the boil, cover the pan and cook gently, stirring occasionally, for 30 minutes or until the fruit is tender.

Allow to cool until the muslin is cool enough to handle, then squeeze out all the juice from the peelings into the pan. Add the lemon juice and sugar to the pan and heat gently to boiling point, stirring continuously until the sugar has dissolved.

Bring to a rolling boil and boil hard to setting point. Stir in the butter to disperse the scum and pot the jam in warmed jars. Cover the surface of the jam with waxed discs, waxed side down, and allow to cool. Top with lids or pieces of cellophane when quite cold.

Apple and Damson Jam

*Damsons give a tangy, well-flavoured jam which is very good
with the mild, crumbly British cheeses such as Lancashire,
Caerphilly and Wensleydale.*

Makes about 2.25 kg/5 lb

450 g/1 lb cooking apples
1 kg/2 lb damsons
juice of 2 lemons
300 ml/$\frac{1}{2}$ pint water
1.5 kg/3 lb sugar
25 g/1 oz butter

Peel, core and slice the cooking apples, reserving all the peelings
and trimmings. Rinse the damsons, removing any stalks or
damaged fruit. Place the apples and damsons in a large saucepan
and sprinkle the lemon juice over them.

Place the apple trimmings in a small saucepan and pour in the
water. Bring to the boil and cover the pan. Reduce the heat and
simmer for 15 minutes, then press the pulp and the liquid
through a fine sieve over the fruit.

Bring the fruit to the boil, cover the pan and reduce the heat.
Simmer for about 20 minutes, stirring occasionally, until the
apples and damsons are soft. Add the sugar and heat gently,
stirring continuously, until the sugar has dissolved. Bring to a
rapid boil and boil hard to setting point. While the fruit is
boiling, the stones from the damsons will rise to the surface of
the jam and you can skim them off with a slotted spoon.

Stir in the butter and pot the jam in warmed jars. Top each
with a disc of waxed paper, waxed side down, and allow to cool.
Cover the jars when completely cold.

Cherry and Apple Jam

(Illustrated on page 34)

Both sweet and bitter cherries are suitable for this jam. If you want to make a very special preserve, stir 4–6 tablespoons brandy into the jam before you pot it.

Makes about 2.25 kg/5 lb

1 kg/2 lb cherries
1 kg/2 lb cooking apples
juice of 2 lemons
1 15 litres/2 pints water
1 25 kg/2½ lb sugar
15 g/½ oz butter

Stone the cherries and place the stones in a large saucepan. Peel, core and thickly slice the cooking apples, then sprinkle the slices with the lemon juice and set them aside. Add the apple trimmings to the pan with the cherry stones and pour in the water. Bring to the boil and cook, uncovered, until the liquid is reduced to about one-third of its original quantity – this should take about 1 hour.

Press the resulting pulp through a fine sieve and return it to the rinsed-out saucepan. Add the prepared cherries and apple and bring the mixture to the boil. Cover the pan and simmer gently, stirring occasionally, for 10–15 minutes, until the fruit is soft.

Pour in the sugar and heat gently, stirring, until the sugar has dissolved. Bring the jam to a rapid boil and boil hard to setting point. Stir in the butter to disperse any scum and pot the jam into warmed jars. Cover the surfaces with waxed paper discs, waxed sides down, and allow to cool. Top the pots with cellophane covers or lids and label them when cold.

Apricot and Date Jam

(Illustrated on page 33)

Home-made apricot jam is superbly flavoured, leaving the supermarket varieties well in the shade.

Makes about 1.5 kg/3 lb

1 kg/2 lb fresh apricots
225 g/8 oz fresh dates
600 ml/1 pint water
grated rind of 1 orange
1.25 kg/2½ lb sugar
25 g/1 oz butter

Halve and stone the apricots. Crack the stones and take out the kernels. Place the fruit and their kernels in a large saucepan. Halve and stone the dates, removing and discarding their skins, and place them in the saucepan. Pour in the water, add the orange rind and bring to the boil. Reduce the heat and simmer the fruit, uncovered, for 30 minutes.

Add the sugar to the jam and stir it over a low heat until the sugar has completely dissolved. Bring to the boil and boil rapidly until setting point is reached. Add the butter to the pan, stirring it in to disperse the scum.

Pot the jam in warmed pots and cover the surface of each with a disc of waxed paper, waxed side down. Leave to cool, then cover the pots and label them.

Winter Apricot Jam

This is a recipe for dried fruit—useful for the winter months when home-made jam is especially welcome. Try serving it with warm croissants for breakfast or toasted muffins and clotted cream at teatime.

Makes about 1.75 kg/3 lb

450 g/1 lb dried apricots
600 ml/1 pint water
1 kg/2 lb sugar
3 lemons
15 g/½ oz butter

Put the apricots in a large saucepan and pour in the water. Leave them to soak for about 3–4 hours. Bring to the boil, cover the pan and reduce the heat, then simmer the fruit for about 30 minutes or until tender.

Add the sugar. Squeeze the juice from the lemons and add it to the pan together with the squeezed-out lemon shells, taking care to remove the pips first. Stir over gentle heat until the sugar has completely dissolved, then bring to the boil and boil hard to setting point.

Remove the lemon shells from the jam and stir in the butter to disperse any scum. Pour the jam into warmed pots and top with waxed discs, waxed sides down. Allow to cool, then cover the jars with lids or pieces of cellophane when quite cold.

Apricot and Loganberry Jam

(Illustrated on page 34)

The loganberry is thought to be a cross between a raspberry and a blackberry. Here, it combines with apricots to give a luscious jam which turns the simplest of cakes into a special treat.
As well as filling cakes, try this jam with your favourite dessert: mix a little into a plain apple tart, layer it with cold, creamy rice pudding, or treat the family to a superior jam roly-poly.

Makes about 2.25 kg/5 lb

1 kg/2 lb fresh apricots
300 ml/$\frac{1}{2}$ pint water
450 g/1 lb loganberries
1.5 kg/3 lb sugar
25 g/1 oz butter

Halve and stone the apricots. Crack the stones and remove the kernels. Mix the fruit with their kernels in a large saucepan and pour in the water. Bring to the boil and reduce the heat, then cook the apricots, uncovered, for 5–10 minutes until they are just soft.

Add the loganberries to the pan and gradually stir in the sugar. Stir the mixture over a gentle heat until the sugar has dissolved completely, bring it to the boil and boil hard until setting point is reached.

Stir in the butter to disperse the scum and transfer the jam to warmed pots. Cover with waxed discs, waxed sides down, and leave to cool completely. Top the pots with pieces of cellophane or airtight lids and label them neatly.

Strawberry and Peach Jam

Choose ripe, well-flavoured peaches for this delicate jam. Use it to fill light sponge cakes, warm scones or pancakes.

Makes 2.75 kg/6 lb

450 g/1 lb cooking apples
1 lemon
6 large ripe peaches
900 ml/1½ pints water
1 kg/2 lb strawberries
1.75 kg/4 lb sugar
25 g/1 oz butter

Rinse and dry the apples, then chop them up, stalk, pips, core and all. Squeeze the juice from the lemon and finely chop the remainder of it. Mix the apples and lemon together with the juice in a large saucepan.

Place the peaches in a large bowl and cover them with boiling water. Leave to stand for 1 minute, then drain and peel them. Place the peel in the saucepan. Stone the peaches, crack the stones and add them to the apples in the pan. Pour in the water and bring the mixture to the boil. Boil, uncovered, for 10 minutes, stirring occasionally, until the fruit is reduced to a pulpy mixture.

Slice the peach flesh into a large saucepan. Hull the strawberries and add them to the pan with the peaches. Press the cooked apple mixture through a fine sieve into the pan, bring the mixture to the boil and simmer it for about 5–10 minutes, until the fruit is soft.

Add the sugar to the pan and stir over a gentle heat until the sugar has dissolved completely. Bring to the boil and boil hard to setting point. Stir in the butter to disperse the scum and transfer the jam to warmed pots. Cover each with a disc of waxed paper, waxed side down, and allow to cool. Top with lids or pieces of cellophane when completely cold.

Raspberry and Redcurrant Jam

This piquantly sharp jam can sometimes contain rather a lot of seeds. If you do not like too many seeds in jam, then cook half the fruit separately and press it through a sieve before adding it to the remaining fruit.

Makes about 1.5 kg/3 lb

450 g/1 lb raspberries
450 g/1 lb redcurrants
300 ml/$\frac{1}{2}$ pint water
juice of 2 lemons
1 kg/2 lb sugar
25 g/1 oz butter

Mix the fruit in a large saucepan and add the water. Bring to the boil, cover the pan and simmer for about 20–30 minutes, until the redcurrants are really tender.

Add the lemon juice and sugar and stir over a gentle heat until the sugar has dissolved completely. Bring to a rapid boil and boil hard to setting point. Stir in the butter and transfer the jam to warmed pots.

Cover the surface of the jam with waxed discs, waxed sides down, and allow to cool, then cover the pots with lids or pieces of cellophane. Label and store.

Gooseberry and Peach Jam

Choose gooseberries which are not quite ripe, since they contain the most pectin. For the best flavour the peaches should be ripe.

Makes about 1.75 kg/4 lb

1 kg/2 lb gooseberries
12 peaches
300 ml/$\frac{1}{2}$ pint water
juice of 3 lemons
1.5 kg/3 lb sugar
25 g/1 oz butter

Top and tail the gooseberries and place them in a saucepan. Place the peaches in a large bowl and cover them with boiling water. Allow to stand for 1 minute, then drain and peel them. Cut the peaches in half, remove their stones and slice the fruit into the pan. Tie the stones and peel up in a piece of muslin and place it in the pan with the fruit. Pour in the water and bring to the boil. Cover the pan, reduce the heat and simmer the fruit for about 30 minutes, stirring occasionally, until the gooseberries are tender.

Allow to cool until the muslin is cold enough to handle, then remove it from the pan and squeeze all the juices out of it back into the fruit.

Add the lemon juice and sugar. Stir the jam over a gentle heat until the sugar has dissolved completely, then bring it to a rapid boil and boil hard to setting point.

Stir in the butter and pour the jam into warmed pots. Cover the surface of the preserve with waxed discs, waxed sides down, and allow to cool. Top the pots with lids or pieces of cellophane when quite cold. Label neatly before storing.

Pear and Date Jam

This sets softly with a thick consistency – a jam for spreading in sandwiches with cream cheese or on slices of hot buttered toast.

Makes about 2.25 kg/5 lb

1 kg/2 lb pears
450 g/1 lb cooking apples
225 g/8 oz fresh dates
900 ml/1$\frac{1}{2}$ pints water
juice of 2 lemons
1.5 kg/3 lb sugar
15 g/$\frac{1}{2}$ oz butter

Peel, core and slice the pears, setting them aside, and place all the trimmings in a large saucepan. Rinse and dry the apples and chop them. Halve the dates, remove the stones and skin and place these trimmings in the pan with the pear trimmings. Add the chopped apples followed by the water and bring to the boil. Cover and boil for 20–30 minutes, stirring occasionally, until the apples are reduced to a pulp.

Press the boiled mixture through a fine sieve into a large saucepan. Add the slices of pear and halved dates. Pour in the lemon juice and bring to the boil, then cover the pan, reduce the heat and simmer, stirring from time to time, for about 30 minutes, until the fruit is softened.

Add the sugar to the pan and stir the jam over a low heat until the sugar has completely dissolved. Bring to the boil and boil hard until setting point is reached. Stir in the butter and transfer the jam to warmed pots. Cover the surfaces with waxed discs, waxed sides down, and leave until cold. Top the pots with lids or pieces of cellophane and label when quite cold.

NOTE If you like spiced jam this is a good preserve to spice as the flavours of the fruit are accentuated and warmed by the addition of a cinnamon stick, a few cloves and about 2 tablespoons grated fresh root ginger. Add these spices to the apples while they are boiling and continue as above.

Plum and Orange Jam

Here is a tangy jam with a good colour and flavour. It is important to choose hard plums as these contain enough pectin for the jam to set.

Makes about 2.75 kg/6 lb

1.75 kg/4 lb hard plums
grated rind and juice of 2 small oranges
1.75 kg/4 lb sugar
25 g/1 oz butter

Cut the plum flesh off the stones and roughly chop it. Crack about 20 of the stones, take out the kernels and place them in a large saucepan with the chopped plums, orange rind and juice and about 25 g/1 oz of the sugar.

Bring to the boil, then simmer gently over a low heat until the fruit is softened – this should only take about 5 minutes. Add the remaining sugar to the pan and heat slowly, stirring continuously, until the sugar melts completely. Bring to a rapid, rolling boil and boil hard to setting point. Remove some of the scum from the surface of the jam with a slotted spoon, then stir in the butter and pour the jam into warmed pots.

Cover with waxed discs, waxed sides down, and allow to cool. Top with lids or pieces of cellophane when completely cold. Label and store in a cool place.

Apple and Mandarin Jam

(Illustrated on page 34)

The mandarins make this a very well-flavoured jam with an excellent set. Removing all the pips from the fruit takes a little effort, but the resulting flavour is worth the trouble.

Makes about 1 kg/2 lb

450 g/1 lb mandarins
450 g/1 lb cooking apples
600 ml/1 pint water
juice of 2 lemons
800 g/1$\frac{3}{4}$ lb sugar

Halve the mandarins and carefully remove all the pips. Chop the flesh and the peel quite finely, removing any further pips. Peel, core and slice the apples. Mix the apple peelings and cores with the pips from the mandarins and tie them securely in a piece of clean muslin.

Put all the chopped fruit in a large saucepan and pour in the water. Add the muslin package and bring to the boil. Cover the pan, reduce the heat and simmer the mixture gently for 1 hour, or until the fruit is soft.

Allow to cool until the muslin can be handled, then squeeze all the juices out of it into the jam. Pour in the lemon juice and sugar and heat the jam gently, stirring continuously, until the sugar has completely dissolved. Bring it to the boil and boil hard to setting point.

Pour the jam into warmed pots and top each with a waxed disc, waxed side down. Allow to cool before covering the pots with lids or pieces of cellophane.

Melon and Ginger Jam

This is delicately flavoured and sets firmly. Serve it with very thin slices of bread and butter.

Makes 1.5 kg/3 lb

1 ripe honeydew melon
450 g/1 lb cooking apples
75 g/3 oz fresh root ginger
1.15 litres/2 pints water
juice of 3 lemons
1 kg/2 lb sugar
25 g/1 oz butter

Halve the melon, scoop out the seeds and place them in a large saucepan. Cut the melon into quarters and cut out the flesh, putting it aside. Chop all the peel and place it in the pan with the seeds. Rinse and dry the apples, chop them and add them to the pan. Coarsely grate the ginger and put it in the pan, then pour in the water and bring to the boil. Continue to boil, covered, for 30 minutes, then press the mixture through a sieve.

Chop the reserved melon flesh and simmer it in the sieved liquid for about 15 minutes in a covered pan. Add the lemon juice and sugar and cook over a low heat, stirring continuously until the sugar has dissolved. Bring to the boil and boil hard to setting point.

Stir in the butter and transfer the jam to warmed pots. Cover with discs of waxed paper, waxed sides down, and leave until cold. Top the pots with lids or pieces of cellophane and label clearly.

Tropical Fruit Jam

Perhaps a little expensive but certainly delectable, this jam is well worth the effort required in the preparation of the coconut. Serve it with hot, thick Scotch pancakes, or as a filling for fine crêpes or a sweet mille feuilles.

Makes about 1.5 kg/3 lb

1 pineapple
1 coconut
6 limes
2 cooking apples
1.75 litres/3 pints water
1 kg/2 lb sugar
25 g/1 oz butter

Cut the top off the pineapple, chop the leaves and place them in a large saucepan. Peel and trim the pineapple, removing all the eyes. Chop the trimmings and place them in the saucepan. Chop the flesh and core of the fruit and set them aside.

Pierce the eyes of the coconut and drain the liquid into the pan. Break the shell and remove all the flesh. Coarsely grate the coconut flesh and add it to the other trimmings in the pan. Grate the rind off the limes and mix it in a bowl with the reserved pineapple flesh. Squeeze the juice from the limes and chop the remaining shells: add both to the pan.

Finally, rinse, dry and chop the apples and put them in the pan before pouring in the water. Bring to the boil, cover the pan and cook for 2 hours at a steady simmer. Allow to cool. Strain the mixture into a clean pan, pressing the juice out of the trimmings.

Put the pineapple flesh and lime rind into the pan and bring to the boil; cover the pan, reduce the heat and simmer the fruit for 15 minutes. Stir in the sugar until dissolved, then bring the jam to the boil and boil hard to setting point. Stir in the butter to disperse the scum and pot immediately into warmed jars. Top each pot of jam with a waxed disc, waxed side down. Allow to cool, then cover with lids or pieces of cellophane.

NOTE If you cannot find a fresh coconut in your local greengrocer or supermarket, substitute a 225-g/8-oz packet of coconut cream for it and continue as above.

Pineapple and Passionfruit Jam

The combination of two exotic fruits creates a very special jam. The addition of cooking apples provides extra bulk without diminishing the superb flavour.

Makes about 1.75 kg/4 lb

1 large ripe pineapple
675 g/1½ lb cooking apples
6 passionfruit
1.15 litres/2 pints water
1.5 kg/3 lb sugar
juice of 2 large lemons

Peel the pineapple and roughly chop the peel together with any leaves. Rinse and roughly chop the whole apples and cut the passionfruit into quarters. Place all these prepared ingredients in a large saucepan and pour in the water. Bring to the boil, cover the pan and reduce the heat. Simmer for 1 hour.

Meanwhile, chop the pineapple flesh, cutting up the hard core more finely than the soft part of the fruit. Place this prepared fruit in a large saucepan. Press the cooked pulp through a fine sieve and pour the resulting purée into the pan with the pineapple. Bring the fruit mixture slowly to the boil, cover the pan and simmer the fruit for 30 minutes or until quite tender.

Add the sugar and lemon juice and stir the jam over a gentle heat until the sugar has completely dissolved. Bring it to the boil and boil hard to setting point. Transfer the jam to warmed pots, top each with a disc of waxed paper, waxed side down, and allow to cool. Cover the cooled pots with lids or pieces of cellophane.

Crab-apple Jelly

This slightly sharp jelly is always popular for its delightful colour and flavour. Good on hot buttered toast, it also makes the perfect accompaniment to roast pork, ham or gammon steaks.
It is difficult to estimate either the quantity of sugar needed to make basic jellies or the yields, as these depend on the quantity of the fruit and the amount of juice it contains.

1.75 kg/4 lb crab-apples
1.15 litres/2 pints water
juice of 2 lemons
4 cloves
sugar

Rinse and roughly chop the crab-apples, place them in a saucepan and add the water and lemon juice. Stir in the cloves and bring to the boil. Cover the pan, lower the heat and simmer the fruit for about 1½ hours, until reduced to a pulp.

Allow to cool slightly, then strain the mixture overnight through a jelly bag. Measure the resulting liquid and pour it into a large saucepan with 450 g/1 lb sugar for each 600 ml/1 pint. Heat slowly to boiling point, stirring continuously until the sugar dissolves. Bring to a rapid boil and boil hard to setting point. Skim the surface with a slotted spoon and pot the jelly in warmed jars. Cover the surfaces with waxed discs, waxed sides down, and allow to cool. Top with lids or cellophane covers when completely cold.

Apricot and Date Jam (page 20)

Apricot and
Date Jam

Apricot and
Date Jam

Damson Jelly

An old favourite, damson jelly is often considered easier to prepare than damson jam since the stones are removed when the fruit is strained instead of having to be skimmed off during the boiling process.

1.5 kg/3 lb damsons
2 lemons
900 ml/1½ pints water
sugar

Remove any stalks and damaged areas from the fruit and place it in a large saucepan. Squeeze the lemons and add the juice to the pan. Chop the remainder of the lemons and put them in the pan too. Pour over the water and bring to the boil. Cover the pan and reduce the heat, then simmer for about 1½ hours until the fruit is reduced to a pulp.

Strain the slightly cooled fruit overnight through a jelly bag. Measure the extract and allow 450 g/1 lb sugar to each 600 ml/1 pint. Pour the liquid and sugar into a large saucepan and heat the mixture gently, stirring, until the sugar has dissolved completely. Bring it to a rapid boil and boil hard to setting point.

Remove the scum from the surface with a slotted spoon and pour the jelly into warmed jars. Cover the surface of the preserve with discs of waxed paper, waxed side down and allow to cool. Cover the jars with lids or pieces of cellophane and label.

Clockwise from the top: Apricot and Loganberry Jam (page 22); Apple and Mandarin Jam (page 28); Cherry and Apple Jam (page 19); Blackcurrant Butter (page 49); Lemon Curd (page 53).

Blackcurrant Jelly

This full-flavoured jelly will taste very good with scones and cream.

450 g/1 lb cooking apples
450 g/1 lb blackcurrants
600 ml/1 pint water
2 large lemons
about 1.5 kg/3 lb sugar

Chop the apples, including the peel and cores. Place them in a saucepan with the blackcurrants and water. Squeeze the juice from the lemons and add it to the pan. Chop the remainder of the lemons and add them to the fruit, then bring to the boil and simmer over a low heat, covered, for 1 hour.

Allow to cool and strain the mixture overnight through a jelly bag. Measure the resulting juice and put it in a large pan with 450 g/1 lb sugar for each 600 ml/1 pint of the juice extract. Heat slowly to boiling point, stirring continuously until the sugar has dissolved.

Bring to a rolling boil and boil the jelly hard to setting point. Carefully skim the scum off the surface, using a slotted spoon. Pour the jelly into warmed pots, cover the surface with waxed discs, waxed sides down, and allow to cool. Top the jelly with cellophane covers or lids and label neatly before storing.

Redcurrant Jelly

This preserve is traditionally served with roast lamb. It is also one of the ingredients for a Cumberland sauce – a mixture of orange juice, rind and red wine with redcurrant jelly. Why not try it, too, with cold roast meats or use it as you would any other sweet preserve?

1 kg/2 lb redcurrants
600 ml/1 pint water
1 large lemon
sugar

Trim any leaves off the redcurrants and place the fruit with all its stalks in a saucepan. Pour in the water. Squeeze the juice from the lemon and add it to the pan. Chop the remainder of the lemon and put it in too.

Bring to the boil, cover the pan and reduce the heat. Simmer the fruit for 1½ hours, until it is very pulpy. Allow to cool slightly before straining it through a jelly bag, preferably overnight.

Measure the extract and allow 450 g/1 lb sugar to each 600 ml/ 1 pint. Pour the liquid into a clean pan and add the measured sugar. Stirring continuously, heat gently until the sugar has dissolved completely, then bring to a rapid boil and boil hard to setting point.

Skim the surface of the jelly and pour it into warmed pots. Top each with a disc of waxed paper, waxed side down, and allow to cool before covering with lids or pieces of cellophane.

NOTE This jelly is delicious spiced. Add a cinnamon stick and a few cloves, if liked, to the fruit as it is boiling.

Bramble Jelly

Here is an old favourite which is always worth the effort involved as it gives such an excellent flavour. The juice content of the fruit varies so much that, as with other basic jellies, it is not practical to give a yield for this recipe.

2.25 kg/5 lb blackberries
3 lemons
600 ml/1 pint water
sugar

Pick over and rinse the blackberries. Place them in a large saucepan. Squeeze the juice from the lemons and add it to the pan. Chop the remainder of the lemons and stir them into the blackberries.

Pour in the water and bring to the boil. Reduce the heat, cover the pan and simmer the fruit for $1-1\frac{1}{2}$ hours, until reduced to a pulp. Allow to cool, strain through a jelly bag overnight and measure the resulting extract.

Pour the extract into a large saucepan and add 450 g/1 lb sugar for each 600 ml/1 pint. Heat slowly until the sugar has dissolved, stirring continuously, then bring to a rapid boil and boil hard to setting point.

Skim the surface of the jelly with a slotted spoon to remove all the scum and pour it into warmed jars. Cover the surfaces with waxed discs, waxed sides down, and allow to cool. Top the pots with lids or pieces of cellophane.

Mint Jelly

This is a traditional way of preserving mint for use in the very early spring or winter months. You can also make jellies flavoured with other fresh herbs; for example, try using rosemary instead of mint, or a selection of mixed herbs.

Makes about 1.5–1.75 kg/3–4 lb

1.75 kg/4 lb cooking apples
300 ml/½ pint white vinegar
600 ml/1 pint water
1.5 kg/3 lb sugar
100 g/4 oz fresh mint

Rinse and chop the apples, then place them in a saucepan with the vinegar and water. Bring to the boil, cover the pan and simmer the fruit for 1 hour. Allow to cool slightly before straining it through a jelly bag overnight.

Pour the extract or juices from the fruit into a large saucepan and add the sugar. Stir gently over a low heat until the sugar has dissolved, then bring to a rapid boil and boil hard to setting point.

Meanwhile, pick the leaves from the mint and chop them finely. Skim the surface of the boiled jelly and stir in the mint. Allow to stand for 10 minutes, stir well and pour into warmed jars.

Cover the surface of the jelly with waxed discs, waxed sides down, then allow to cool before covering with lids or pieces of cellophane.

Lemon Mint Jelly

The combination of lemon and mint makes a tangy jelly which is perfect for serving with hot or cold roast lamb, boiled new potatoes and peas or with a lightly dressed cucumber salad.

Makes about 675 g/1½ lb

3 large lemons
300 ml/½ pint vinegar
900 ml/1½ pints water
450 g/1 lb sugar
100 g/4 oz fresh mint

Chop the lemons and place them in a saucepan with the vinegar and water. Bring to the boil, then cover the pan and reduce the heat. Simmer the fruit for 1½ hours. Allow to cool and strain it overnight through a jelly bag.

Pour the juice into a large saucepan and stir in the sugar. Heat gently, stirring, until the sugar has completely dissolved, then bring to the boil and boil hard to setting point.

Wash the mint while the jelly is boiling and pick off all the leaves. Discard the stalks and finely chop the leaves. Carefully skim the surface of the boiled jelly with a slotted spoon to remove the scum and add the mint. Stir it in and leave to stand for about 10 minutes. Transfer the jelly to warmed pots, cover the surfaces with waxed discs, waxed sides down, and allow to cool. Cover the pots of cold jelly with lids or pieces of cellophane.

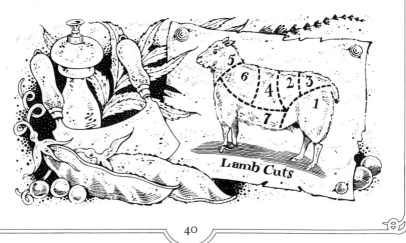

Lamb Cuts

Spiced Orange Jelly

Serve this sweet jelly with fresh fruit – halved and stoned fresh peaches, strawberries, raspberries and others. It can also be mixed with natural yogurt or whipped cream for a quick dessert, or served as a topping for ice cream.

Makes 1.5 kg/3 lb

675 g/1½ lb cooking apples
4 large oranges
1 large lemon
1.75 litres/3 pints water
6 cloves
1 cinnamon stick
about 1 kg/2¼ lb sugar

Rinse and dry the apples, then chop them and place them in a large saucepan. Chop the whole oranges and the lemon and add them to the pan. Pour in the water and add the spices. Bring to the boil, cover the pan and reduce the heat. Simmer the fruit for 1 hour. Allow it to cool and strain it through a jelly bag overnight.

Measure the juice and add 450 g/1 lb sugar for each 600 ml/ 1 pint. Heat the mixture gently in a large saucepan over a low heat, stirring until the sugar has completely dissolved. Bring to the boil and boil hard to setting point.

Carefully skim the surface of the jelly with a slotted spoon to remove the scum, pour it into hot jars and top each with a disc of waxed paper, waxed side down. Allow to cool. Cover and label the pots when cold.

Orange and Raspberry Jelly

*This summery fruit jelly will enhance all kinds of desserts, from
the simple to the spectacular. For a very quick dessert, serve it
layered in glasses with whipped cream and natural yogurt.
Or, for more special occasions, serve a little jelly on each glass of
syllabub, or with each portion of coeur à la crème.*

Makes about 1.5 kg/3 lb

450 g/1 lb cooking apples
4 oranges
1 lemon
450 g/1 lb raspberries
1.75 litres/3 pints water
1.25 kg/2½ lb sugar

Wash and dry the cooking apples. Chop them and place them in
a large saucepan. Chop the oranges and lemon and add them to
the pan together with the raspberries and water. Bring to the
boil and cover the pan, then simmer the fruit for 1 hour.

Allow to cool before straining the mixture overnight through
a jelly bag. Pour the strained juices into a large saucepan and add
the sugar. Stir over a low heat until the sugar has dissolved, then
bring to a rolling boil and boil to setting point.

Skim the surface of the jelly with a slotted spoon to remove the
scum, then pour it into hot jars and cover with waxed discs,
waxed sides down. Allow to set. Cover the cold jelly with lids
or pieces of cellophane.

Grape and Port Jelly

This is a soft-setting jelly which should be stored in a cool place. It has an excellent flavour and will complement any home-made ice cream, vanilla mousse or delicate cheesecake.

Makes about 1.5 kg/3 lb

1 kg/2 lb black grapes
3 lemons
1.75 litres/3 pints water
about 675 g/1½ lb sugar
150 ml/¼ pint port

Rinse the grapes under running water. Halve and place them in a large saucepan with their stalks. Squeeze and reserve the juice from the lemons. Chop the remainder of the lemons and place them in the pan with the grapes and the water. Bring to the boil, reduce the heat and cover the pan. Simmer for 1 hour and allow to cool. Strain the mixture through a jelly bag overnight.

Measure the resulting juice and pour it into a clean pan. Add 350 g/12 oz sugar to each 600 ml/1 pint of liquid. Pour in the port and lemon juice and stir over a low heat until the sugar has dissolved. Bring to the boil and boil steadily until setting point is reached. Carefully skim any scum off the jelly and pot it in warmed jars. Top each jar with a disc of waxed paper, waxed side down, and allow to cool. Cover the cold jelly with lids or pieces of cellophane.

Fruit Butters
and Conserves

THESE are rather special preserves to be made either when there is an abundance of superior fruit on the market, or when you want to make up a delicacy in small quantities and keep it for special occasions.

Fruit butters take larger quantities of fruit than jams and reduce it to a concentrated, smooth and sweet preserve. They can be used to spread lightly on bread and butter, scones or toast. They are called butters because of their creamy consistency; this is achieved by sieving the cooked fruit and boiling the resulting pulp with sugar until thick.

Conserves are whole fruit preserves of a syrupy nature – they are not set, but thick. They can be poured over desserts – cream moulds and custards, sponge puddings and pies – or used in flans and gâteaux. Often enriched with liqueurs or spirits, they are definitely looked upon as a favourite treat and are fun to prepare for a special gift.

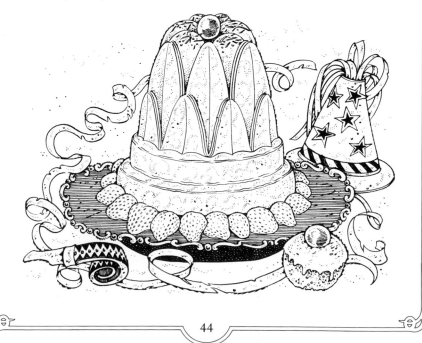

Spiced Apple Butter

Windfall apples are ideal for this preserve. Cut out any bad parts, rinse the apples, but do not bother to peel them as the cooked fruit will have to be sieved anyway.

Makes about 1.5 kg/3 lb

1.25 kg/2½ lb cooking apples
1 cinnamon stick
1 teaspoon nutmeg
1 lemon, chopped
600 ml/1 pint water
about 575 g/1¼ lb sugar

Rinse and roughly chop the apples and place them in a saucepan with the spices, chopped lemon and water. Bring to the boil, cover the pan and reduce the heat. Simmer for 1 hour, or until the fruit is reduced to a pulp.

Press the mixture through a fine sieve, weigh the resulting purée and put it in a clean pan. Add 350 g/12 oz sugar to each 450 g/1 lb of purée and stir over a low heat until the sugar has completely dissolved. Bring to the boil and boil steadily for about 30 minutes, until the mixture is reduced by half and is thick and creamy. Remember to stir it frequently during cooking to prevent it from sticking to the pan and burning.

Transfer the butter to warmed pots and cover with discs of waxed paper, waxed sides down. Leave to cool, and top with lids or pieces of cellophane.

Plum and Apple Butter

Spread rich, sweet butters in small quantities on sponges for making a trifle, or warm the butter and thin it down with a little dry sherry to make a superb fruit sauce for steamed puddings.

Makes about 1.75 kg/4 lb

1 kg/2 lb plums
1 kg/2 lb cooking apples
600 ml/1 pint water
about 1 kg/2 lb sugar

Place the plums in a large pan. Roughly chop the apples and add them to the plums together with the water. Bring to the boil, then cover the pan and reduce the heat so that the fruit simmers steadily for about $1-1\frac{1}{2}$ hours. It should be reduced to a pulp.

Press the pulp through a fine sieve and weigh it. Put it in a clean pan and add 350 g/12 oz sugar to each 450 g/1 lb pulp. Heat the pulp slowly, stirring continuously, until the sugar has dissolved. Bring to the boil and continue to boil steadily for about 40 minutes. Stir frequently during cooking to prevent the butter from sticking to the pan. When ready, it should be thick enough for the spoon to leave a ribbon trail on the surface of the mixture when lifted.

Spoon the creamy mixture into hot, clean jars and cover with discs of waxed paper, waxed sides down. Allow to cool, then top the pots with lids or cellophane covers.

Banana Butter

This preserve is a great favourite with children and is delicious in a simple trifle. Make it when bananas are cheap in local markets or when they are being sold off as slightly over-ripe.

Makes 1 kg/2 lb

10 bananas, peeled
juice of 2 lemons
150 ml/$\frac{1}{4}$ pint water
450 g/1 lb sugar
$\frac{1}{4}$ teaspoon ground mixed spice

Slice the bananas into a large saucepan. Add the lemon juice and water and bring to the boil. Cover the pan, reduce the heat and simmer for about 20–30 minutes or until the fruit is reduced to a pulp.

Press the banana pulp through a fine sieve and return it to a clean pan. Add the sugar, gradually stirring it in as you heat the pan gently. Mix in the spice and continue stirring over a low heat until the sugar has completely dissolved. Bring to the boil, lower the heat and simmer the butter steadily for 30–40 minutes, stirring frequently, until reduced by half and quite thick.

Transfer the butter to warmed pots and cover them with small waxed discs, waxed sides down. Top the pots when cool with airtight lids or cellophane covers.

Lemon Pear Butter

Spread thinly on slices of fresh bread and topped with a little clotted cream, this fruit butter is deliciously wicked. If you don't happen to have the clotted cream then use lemon pear butter as you would a jam, only perhaps a little sparingly.

Makes 1 kg/2 lb

1 kg/2 lb pears
300 ml/½ pint water
2 lemons
about 675 g/1½ lb sugar

Rinse the pears and roughly chop them, unpeeled, into a large saucepan. Add the water. Squeeze the juice from the lemons and pour it into the pan. Chop the remainder of the lemons and stir them in too. Bring to the boil, cover the pan and reduce the heat. Simmer for about 1 hour or until the fruit is reduced to a pulp.

Press the pulp through a fine sieve and weigh the resulting mixture. Add 350 g/12 oz sugar for each 450 g/1 lb pulp, return the mixture to the pan and stir it over a low heat until the sugar has completely dissolved. Bring to the boil and simmer steadily for about 45 minutes, stirring frequently, until the butter has thickened to a creamy consistency. Transfer it to warmed jars and top each with a disc of waxed paper, waxed side down. Cover with lids or pieces of cellophane when quite cold.

Blackcurrant Butter

(Illustrated on page 34)

*This is a rich preserve which has such a delicious flavour that you
will find it will be eaten with every slice of hot buttered toast,
spread in every sponge cake and always sampled as an
in-between-meal snack!*

Makes about 1 kg/2 lb

450 g/1 lb cooking apples
1 kg/2 lb blackcurrants
600 ml/1 pint water
sugar
juice of 2 large lemons

Rinse and roughly chop the apples and place them in a large
saucepan with the blackcurrants and water. Bring to the boil,
cover the pan and reduce the heat. Simmer the fruit for 2 hours.

Allow it to cool slightly, then press it through a fine sieve and
weigh the resulting pulp. For each 450 g/1 lb pulp allow 350 g/
12 oz sugar. Return the pulp to the pan with the sugar and
lemon juice and stir the mixture over a gentle heat until the
sugar has dissolved. Bring it to the boil and boil it for 30–40
minutes, stirring frequently, until the butter has thickened to a
creamy consistency and a spoon dipped into it will leave a
ribbon trail on the surface.

Transfer the butter to warmed pots and top each with a disc of
waxed paper, waxed side down. Leave it to cool and cover the
pots with pieces of cellophane or airtight lids.

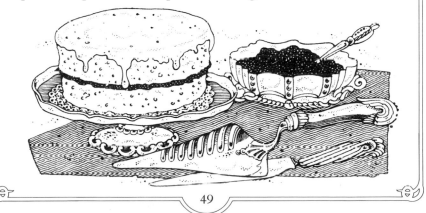

Apricot Butter

If you are lucky enough to have a good fruit market near you, look out for cheap apricots when they are at their most plentiful.

Makes 1.5–1.75 kg/3–4 lb

1.5 kg/3 lb apricots
300 ml/½ pint water
juice of 2 lemons
about 1.5 kg/3 lb sugar

Place the fruit in a saucepan with the water and lemon juice. Bring to the boil, cover the pan and allow to simmer for 1 hour.

Cool slightly before pressing the mixture through a fine sieve. Weigh the resulting pulp and add 350 g/12 oz sugar to each 450 g/1 lb. Put the pulp and sugar in a clean pan and stir the mixture over a low heat until the sugar has dissolved. Then bring it to the boil and boil it steadily, uncovered, for 30–40 minutes, until the butter is thick and creamy. Stir it frequently during cooking to prevent it from sticking to the pan.

Transfer the butter to warmed pots and top each with a waxed disc, waxed side down. Allow to cool completely before covering with lids or pieces of cellophane.

Clockwise from the top: *yogurt with Raspberry and Pear Conserve (page 55);*
vanilla dessert with Cherry Conserve (page 56); cheesecake with Peach Conserve (page 57);
ice cream with Strawberry and Orange Conserve (page 54).

Lemon Curd

(Illustrated on page 34)

Lemon curd is traditionally looked upon as a preserve, and a favourite one at that, two very good reasons for including it here. But it does not have strong keeping properties and should be kept in the refrigerator for not more than 3–4 weeks.

Makes about 1 kg/2 lb

grated rind and juice of 3 large lemons
100 g/4 oz butter, cut into pieces
3 large eggs, beaten
350 g/12 oz caster sugar

Mix all the ingredients in the top of a double saucepan or in a large basin held over a pan of gently simmering water. Do not allow the water to boil or the curd may overheat and curdle.

Stir the mixture until the sugar has dissolved, then continue cooking, stirring frequently, until the eggs are cooked and the mixture has thickened enough to coat the back of a wooden spoon.

Pour the curd into clean, warmed jars and cover the surfaces with waxed paper discs, waxed sides down. Allow to cool before topping the jars with pieces of cellophane or airtight lids.

From the top: *Honey Marmalade (page 70); Dark Orange and Lemon Marmalade (page 64); Ginger Marmalade (page 68); Lime Marmalade (page 69).*

Strawberry and Orange Conserve

(Illustrated on page 51)

This is one of the best preserves for retaining the true flavour of summer fruit. Serve it as a special treat with small meringue nests and clotted cream.

Makes about 1 kg/2 lb

1.5 kg/3 lb strawberries
grated rind and juice of 1 orange
1 kg/2 lb sugar
juice of 3 lemons
4 tablespoons orange liqueur (Cointreau, Curaçao)

Hull 1 kg/2 lb of strawberries and place them in a large bowl with the orange rind and juice. Sprinkle over the sugar and lemon juice and toss the fruit lightly to coat it thoroughly with the sugar. Leave it to stand for two days, preferably in the refrigerator.

Put the soaked fruit in a large saucepan and bring it slowly to the boil. Boil it for 20 minutes, stirring frequently to prevent it from sticking to the pan. Stir in the remaining strawberries, return the conserve to the boil and pour in the liqueur. Transfer the conserve to warmed pots and cover these immediately with waxed paper discs and airtight lids.

Raspberry and Pear Conserve

(Illustrated on page 51)

Serve this luxurious conserve with meringues, ice cream and custard tarts. Why not try a little in your bowl of breakfast porridge?

Makes about 2.25 kg/5 lb

1 kg/2 lb cooking pears
1 kg/2 lb raspberries
1.5 kg/3 lb sugar
25 g/1 oz butter

Peel, core and slice the pears. Layer them with half the raspberries and 1 kg/2 lb of the sugar in a bowl. Leave the fruit to soak overnight.

Pour the soaked fruit and the remaining sugar into a saucepan and bring to the boil, stirring until the sugar has dissolved. Reduce the heat and boil the mixture gently, uncovered, for 1 hour, stirring occasionally. Add the remaining raspberries, return the conserve to the boil and cook for 1 minute. Stir in the butter and transfer the conserve to hot jars. Cover each immediately with a disc of waxed paper and an airtight lid.

Cherry Conserve

(Illustrated on page 51)

*Make this delicious conserve with sour cherries and save it to serve
with very special desserts; use it to fill a sponge flan, top a
creamy vanilla mousse or pour over individual semolina moulds.
It can also be made with sweet cherries but the recipe will then
need the addition of the juice of 4 large lemons.*

Makes about 1.5 kg/3 lb

1 kg/2 lb sour cherries (morello or Montmercy)
1 kg/2 lb sugar
150 ml/$\frac{1}{4}$ pint brandy or orange liqueur
(Cointreau, Curaçao)

Stone the cherries (this is easier with the help of a friend or
relation!). Place the stoned fruit in a large saucepan and add the
sugar. Pour in the brandy or liqueur and stir the mixture over a
low heat until the sugar has dissolved. Heat the conserve to
boiling point, then lower the heat and simmer it gently, stirring
from time to time, until it is reduced to about two-thirds of its
original volume. This will take about 1 hour in an uncovered
pan.

 Pour the conserve into warmed jars and cover these
immediately with waxed paper discs and airtight lids. Allow it
to mature for about 1 month.

Peach Conserve

(Illustrated on page 51)

A good time to make this conserve is when peaches are at their best and cheapest in the shops. Add brandy if you want to make it very special – it gives the cooked fruit a superb flavour.
Serve peach conserve as a topping for fresh raspberries, a sauce for mousses and moulds or as a filling for fine crêpes or sweet soufflé omelettes.

Makes 675 g–1 kg/1½–2 lb

12 peaches
1 kg/2 lb sugar
6 tablespoons brandy (optional)

Place the peaches in a large bowl and cover them with boiling water. Leave to stand for 1 minute, drain and peel the fruit, reserving the skins. Halve and stone the peaches, cracking the stones and reserving both these and the kernels they contain.

Place the fruit skins, stones and kernels in a saucepan and add just enough water to cover them. Bring to the boil and boil until the water is reduced to a shallow layer in the base of the pan. Remove the pan from the heat and press the contents through a fine sieve.

Slice the peach halves quite thickly and put three-quarters of them in a saucepan with the sieved juices from the trimmings and the sugar. Stir the mixture over a low heat until the sugar has dissolved, then bring it to the boil and simmer it steadily, stirring occasionally, for 45 minutes, without covering the pan.

Add the remaining fruit and the brandy, if used, to the conserve and bring it once more to the boil. Cook, simmering gently, for 5 minutes, transfer it to hot jars and cover each immediately with a waxed paper disc and an airtight lid.

Gooseberry and Almond Conserve

The almonds add interest to the gooseberries in this conserve.
Serve it as a topping on simple baked apples or as a fruit sauce
with apple pies, rice puddings and ice cream.

Makes about 1.5 kg/3 lb

1 kg/2 lb gooseberries
100 g/4 oz blanched almonds, halved
juice of 3 lemons
300 ml/½ pint water
1 kg/2 lb sugar

Top and tail the fruit and place it in a saucepan with the nuts,
lemon juice and water. Bring to the boil, cover the pan and
simmer for 20 minutes until the fruit is soft. Add the sugar and
stir until dissolved.

Bring the conserve to the boil and boil it uncovered for 20
minutes, stirring occasionally, until thickened to a heavy syrup.
Pour it into hot jars and cover immediately with waxed paper
discs and airtight lids. Label neatly before storing.

Pear and Melon Conserve

*Serve this delicate conserve with chilled custard moulds, home-
made ice creams or simple cheesecakes.
Orange or mint liqueur may be substituted for the port.*

Makes about 1.75 kg/4 lb

1 kg/2 lb pears
1 small ripe honeydew melon
150 ml/$\frac{1}{4}$ pint water
1 kg/2 lb sugar
juice of 3 lemons
5 tablespoons port

Peel, core and thickly slice the pears. Peel the melon and remove
the seeds, then cut it into large chunks. Mix the prepared fruit in
a large saucepan with the water, bring to the boil and cook
gently, covered, for about 10 minutes. The fruit should be
softened but not pulpy.

Gradually stir in the sugar and continue stirring over a low
heat until it has completely dissolved. Stir in the lemon juice and
port, bring the mixture to the boil and simmer gently, stirring
from time to time, for about 30–40 minutes, until the juices
form a thick syrup. Take care not to overcook it or the mixture
will caramelise.

Transfer the conserve to warmed pots and cover these
immediately with waxed paper discs and airtight lids.

Marmalades
and Mincemeats

THE CLASSIC accompaniment to the British breakfast, marmalade has only fairly recently come to be thought of as a special preserve in its own right, separate from jams. Although Seville oranges were available in her day, Mrs Beeton talks of marmalades as preserves made from the pulp, and perhaps the rind, of firmer fruits, for example pineapples and oranges. She paid no particular attention to them and grouped them with other jams and sweet preserves. Over the years, however, the peculiar piquancy of this citrus preserve has made it the perfect complement to toast at breakfast and it is nowadays hardly thought of as a jam – with its teatime associations – at all.

Marmalades need only a little more time and care in their preparation than jams, and you are very likely to gain immediate success with them as they are made from fruits which generally have a high pectin content. As for testing and setting, these follow exactly the same rules as for jams, so refer to page 13 of the Basic Guide to Making Jams and Jellies.

One of the first thoughts for Christmas should be mincemeat – a preserve of long-standing tradition and one which was originally a means of preserving, as the name suggests, minced meat. However, this traditional recipe has evolved into the predominantly sweet preserve we know today. Prepare your mincemeat well in advance of Christmas and allow it to mature thoroughly. Why not try an apricot or honey mincemeat for a change this Christmas?

Fine Seville Marmalade

Seville oranges are only obtainable for a short time in January.
They are extremely bitter and make the best marmalade.

Makes about 3.25 kg/7 lb

1 kg/2 lb Seville oranges
2.25 litres/4 pints water
1.75 kg/4 lb sugar
juice of 3 lemons

Thinly peel the oranges and cut the rind into fine shreds. Halve the fruit and squeeze out the juice, then put the orange juice and rind in a large saucepan with the water. Chop the remainder of the oranges, including the pith, and tie the pieces in a muslin bag. Add this to the pan and bring the mixture slowly to the boil. Cover the pan, reduce the heat and simmer for 2 hours.

Allow the mixture to cool until the muslin can be handled, then squeeze all the juices out of it into the pan and discard the bag. Add the sugar and lemon juice to the pan and heat slowly, stirring, until the sugar dissolves. Bring to the boil and boil hard to setting point. Skim the surface of the marmalade with a slotted spoon to remove any scum and allow it to stand for 15 minutes. Stir it well, pour it into warmed jars and cover the surfaces with waxed discs, waxed sides down.

Allow to cool, then top the jars with cellophane covers or lids and label them neatly.

Spiced Orange Marmalade

This thick, spicy marmalade is particularly welcome on cold winter mornings.

Makes about 3.25 kg/7 lb

1 kg/2 lb Seville oranges
2.25 litres/4 pints water
2 large lemons
1 cinnamon stick
6 cloves
1.75 kg/4 lb sugar

Place the whole oranges in a large saucepan with the water, lemons and spices. Bring to the boil, cover the pan and reduce the heat. Simmer the fruit for $2-2\frac{1}{4}$ hours or until it is very soft. Allow to cool until the fruit is cold enough to handle.

Chop the oranges and lemons, discarding any pips. Strain the cooking liquid to remove the spices and return it to the pan with the chopped fruit. Add the sugar and stir the mixture over a gentle heat until the sugar has completely dissolved. Bring to the boil and boil the marmalade hard until setting point is reached. Carefully skim the surface with a slotted spoon to remove any scum and leave to stand for 15 minutes.

Stir the marmalade and pour it into clean, warmed jars. Cover these with waxed discs, waxed sides down, and leave to cool. Top the cold marmalade with lids or cellophane covers.

Sweet Orange Marmalade

*This is a fine, well-flavoured marmalade made with
sweet oranges.*

Makes 1–1.5 kg/2–3 lb

4 large oranges
2 large lemons
1.15 litres/2 pints water
1 kg/2 lb sugar

Pare the rind from the oranges and lemons and shred it finely.
Squeeze the juice from the fruit and place it in a large pan
together with the shredded rinds. Chop the remainder of the
fruit and tie it up securely with the pips in a piece of muslin. Add
this to the pan, followed by the water.

Bring to the boil, cover the pan and reduce the heat. Simmer
the fruit for 1¼ hours, until the rind is tender. Allow it to cool
until the muslin can be handled, then squeeze all the juices out of
it into the marmalade.

Pour in the sugar and stir the marmalade over a gentle heat
until the sugar has completely dissolved. Bring it to the boil and
boil hard until setting point is reached. Skim the surface with a
wooden spoon to remove any scum and leave it to stand for
about 15 minutes.

Stir the marmalade well to distribute the rind and pour it into
warmed pots. Cover the surfaces with waxed paper discs,
waxed sides down, and leave to cool. Top with pieces of
cellophane or airtight lids when cold.

Dark Orange and Lemon Marmalade

(Illustrated on page 52)

A small proportion of muscovado sugar gives this marmalade a good, rich flavour. For a tangy marmalade use Seville oranges when they are in season.

Makes about 1.75 kg/4 lb

2 large oranges
4 large lemons
1.75 litres/3 pints water
1 kg/2 lb sugar
225 g/8 oz muscovado sugar

Finely chop the fruit, removing the pips, and place it in a large saucepan with the water. Bring to the boil, cover the pan and reduce the heat. Simmer the fruit for 1½ hours.

Add all the sugar to the pan and stir the mixture over a low heat until the sugar has completely dissolved. Bring to a rolling boil and continue to boil until setting point is reached.

Remove the scum from the surface of the marmalade with a slotted spoon and allow it to stand for about 15 minutes. Stir the marmalade, transfer it to heated pots and cover the surfaces with waxed paper discs, waxed sides down. When quite cool, top the marmalade with pieces of cellophane and label the pots.

Three Fruit Marmalade

An old favourite, this marmalade combines three citrus fruits to give a breakfast preserve with an excellent flavour. It is particularly economical as it offers a high yield.

Makes about 2.25 kg/5 lb

2 grapefruit
2 oranges
2 lemons
1.75 litres/3 pints water
2.25 kg/5 lb sugar

Thinly pare the rind from all the fruit and shred it finely Squeeze the juice from the fruit and pour it into a large saucepan with the finely shredded rinds. Chop all the remainder of the fruit, including the pith, and tie it up securely in a piece of clean muslin. Place the muslin bag in the pan and pour in the water.

Bring the mixture to the boil, cover the pan and simmer for about $1\frac{1}{4}$ hours, until the rinds are tender. Remove the pan from the heat and allow it to stand until the muslin is cool enough to handle, then squeeze all the juices out of the muslin into the pan. Add the sugar and stir the marmalade over a low heat until the sugar has completely dissolved. Bring to the boil and boil hard until setting point is reached.

Skim the surface of the marmalade with a slotted spoon to remove any scum and leave it to stand for about 20 minutes. Stir the marmalade to ensure that the fruit rinds are well distributed, then pour it into warmed pots. Cover each with a disc of waxed paper, waxed side down, and leave until cool. Top the cold preserve with cellophane covers or lids and label each pot neatly.

Lemon and Mandarin Marmalade

Thick, fruity and firm with an unusual but superb fruit flavour, this breakfast preserve will make a very special treat with warm wholemeal rolls or scones.

Makes about 1.75 kg/4 lb

1 kg/2 lb mandarins
4 large lemons
3.5 litres/6 pints water
1.5 kg/3 lb sugar

Halve the mandarins and carefully remove all the pips, putting these on one side. Chop the fruit and place it in a large saucepan. Cut the lemons lengthways into eighths and take out any pips, reserving these also. Thinly slice the lemon wedges widthways, add the slices to the pan and pour in the water. Tie all the pips in a small piece of clean muslin and put them in the pan.

Bring the mixture to the boil, cover the pan, reduce the heat and simmer the fruit for 2 hours. Take the pan off the heat and allow it to stand until the muslin is cool enough to handle. Squeeze all the juice out of the muslin into the pan and stir in the sugar. Heat gently, stirring continuously, until the sugar has completely dissolved, then bring the marmalade to the boil and boil it hard to setting point. Skim the surface with a slotted spoon to remove any scum and leave the marmalade to stand for 15 minutes. Stir it well, pot it in warmed jars and top the surfaces with waxed discs, waxed sides down. Allow to cool, then cover the jars with lids or pieces of cellophane.

Melon and Grapefruit Marmalade

These delicately flavoured fruits blend together to make a tangy marmalade, a pleasant change from the usual orange or lemon breakfast preserves.

Makes 2.75–3.25 kg/6–7 lb

4 large grapefruit (slightly underripe)
1 small honeydew melon
3 litres/5 pints water
about 1.75 kg/4 lb sugar
juice of 3 large lemons

Pare and finely shred the rind from the grapefruit. Thinly peel the melon and finely shred the rind. Squeeze the juice from the grapefruit and mix it in a large saucepan with the rinds and the water. Chop all that remains of the grapefruit and tie the chunks up in a clean piece of muslin. Add this to the pan, bring the mixture to the boil and cover the pan. Reduce the heat and simmer the fruit for 2 hours.

Meanwhile, chop the flesh of the melon, discarding the seeds and reserving any juice. Take the pan off the heat and allow it to cool until the muslin can be handled, then squeeze all the juices from it into the pan. Measure the liquid in the pan and add 450 g/1 lb sugar for every 600 ml/1 pint.

Return the pan to the heat and stir the marmalade continuously until the sugar has completely dissolved. Add the chopped melon with all its juice, followed by the lemon juice, bring the mixture to the boil and boil it hard until setting point is reached. Watch the marmalade closely as it may boil over. When the boiling is complete, carefully skim the surface with a slotted spoon to remove all the scum and leave the marmalade to stand for about 15–20 minutes. Stir it well and transfer it to warmed pots. Cover the surfaces with waxed paper discs, waxed sides down, and leave to cool. Top the cool marmalade with lids or pieces of cellophane and label the pots.

Ginger Marmalade

(Illustrated on page 52)

Home-made marmalade is always much nicer than the shop-bought variety and nowhere is this more true than with the slightly unusual preserves. Here is a recipe for a mildly gingered marmalade – if you prefer a hotter awakening to the day, add more ginger to taste.

Makes about 2.25 kg/5 lb

8 lemons
2 large oranges
2.25 litres/4 pints water
100 g/4 oz fresh root ginger
1.5 kg/3 lb sugar

Pare the rind from the lemons and oranges and cut it into thin strips. Squeeze the juice from the fruit and mix it in a large saucepan with the rinds and water. Thinly peel the ginger, slice and finely shred it, then add it to the pan.

Chop the remainder of the lemons and oranges, including the pith, and tie them up in a piece of clean muslin. Add the muslin bag to the pan and bring the mixture to the boil. Reduce the heat, cover the pan and simmer for 2 hours or until the ginger and fruit rinds are completely tender. Take the pan off the heat and leave it to stand until the muslin is cool enough to handle, then squeeze all the juices out of it into the marmalade.

Pour the sugar into the pan and stir the mixture over a gentle heat until the sugar has completely dissolved. Bring to the boil and boil hard to setting point. Use a slotted spoon to remove the scum from the top of the marmalade, then allow it to stand for about 15–20 minutes. Stir it thoroughly before pouring it into warmed pots. Cover with waxed discs, waxed sides down, and allow to cool before topping the pots with lids or cellophane covers.

Lime Marmalade

(Illustrated on page 52)

This is a delicious, slightly tangy and flavoursome marmalade. Although limes are sometimes quite expensive, this marmalade gives a high yield which compensates for the initial cost of the fruit.

Makes 2.25 kg/5 lb

6 limes
2 lemons
1.4 litres/2½ pints water
1.5 kg/3 lb sugar

Cut the limes into quarters lengthways and then into long, very fine slices, removing all the pips. Cut up the lemons in the same way and mix both lots of fruit in a large saucepan. Pour in the water and bring to the boil. Cover the pan, reduce the heat and simmer the fruit for 1½ hours.

Add the sugar to the softened fruit and stir the mixture over a low heat until the sugar has completely dissolved. Bring the marmalade to a rolling boil and continue to boil until setting point is reached.

Remove the scum from the surface of the marmalade with a slotted spoon and leave it to stand for about 10 minutes. Stir it thoroughly before potting it in warmed jars. Top each with a disc of waxed paper, waxed side down, and leave to cool. Cover with pieces of cellophane and label the cold marmalade.

Honey Marmalade

(Illustrated on **page** 52)

Make this marmalade either chunky or fine (see below), whichever you prefer. I use the whole chopped fruit and a little honey to give a well-flavoured, chunky marmalade.

Makes 1.5 kg/3 lb

4 large lemons
1.15 litres/2 pints water
675 g/1½ lb sugar
225 g/8 oz thick honey

Slice the lemons lengthways into quarters, discarding the pips, and cut the quarters widthways into fine slices. Place the fruit in a large saucepan with the water and bring the mixture to the boil. Cover the pan, reduce the heat and simmer for 1¼ hours.

Add the sugar and honey and stir the mixture over a low heat until the sugar has completely dissolved. Bring it to the boil and boil rapidly until setting point is reached.

Carefully remove the scum from the surface of the marmalade with a slotted spoon, then allow it to stand for about 15 minutes. Stir the preserve thoroughly before pouring it into warmed pots. Cover the surfaces immediately with discs of waxed paper, waxed sides down, and leave to cool. Top the cooled marmalade with pieces of cellophane or airtight lids.

NOTE To make a fine marmalade, begin by paring the rind from the lemons and shredding it finely. Squeeze out the juice and place it in the pan with the rind. Chop the remainder of the fruit, tie it securely with the pips in a piece of muslin and add this to the pan. Pour in the water, bring to the boil and continue as above, but before you add the sugar, allow the marmalade to cool until the muslin can be handled. Squeeze the juices from the bag into the marmalade, pour in the sugar and proceed as in the main recipe.

Mincemeat

At one time mincemeat was a mixture of minced meat and dried fruits, but over the years it has become a mixture of suet, dried fruits, apples and brandy or rum.

Makes about 1.75 kg/4 lb

225 g/8 oz raisins
225 g/8 oz sultanas
225 g/8 oz currants
225 g/8 oz shredded suet
100 g/4 oz chopped mixed peel
100 g/4 oz blanched almonds
450 g/1 lb cooking apples
1 large carrot
grated rind and juice of 1 orange
juice of 2 lemons
225 g/8 oz dark soft brown sugar
$\frac{1}{2}$ teaspoon freshly grated nutmeg
$\frac{1}{2}$ teaspoon ground cinnamon
150 ml/$\frac{1}{4}$ pint brandy or rum
4 tablespoons dry sherry

Mince or finely chop the raisins, sultanas and currants and mix them with the suet and peel in a large bowl. Chop the almonds and add them to the fruit. Peel, core and grate the apples and grate the carrot, then stir both into the fruit with the orange rind and juice, the lemon juice and sugar.

Stir in the spices and pour over the brandy or rum and the sherry, mixing thoroughly to combine all the ingredients. Leave the mincemeat to stand for a couple of days, stirring it every day. Transfer it to pots and cover these with airtight lids. Allow the mincemeat to mature for at least 3 weeks before use.

NOTE For an economical mincemeat, use 150 ml/$\frac{1}{4}$ pint sherry and just 4 tablespoons brandy or rum instead of vice versa.

Apricot Mincemeat

Dried apricots and crystallised ginger make a deliciously unusual mincemeat.

Makes about 1.75 kg/4 lb

50 g/2 oz crystallised ginger
225 g/8 oz dried apricots
225 g/8 oz raisins
175 g/6 oz sultanas
175 g/6 oz currants
50 g/2 oz chopped mixed peel
50 g/2 oz blanched almonds, chopped
225 g/8 oz cooking apples
grated rind and juice of 3 oranges
grated rind and juice of 2 lemons
225 g/8 oz soft brown sugar
350 g/12 oz carrots
$\frac{1}{2}$ teaspoon ground mixed spice
$\frac{1}{4}$ teaspoon freshly grated nutmeg
150 ml/$\frac{1}{4}$ pint brandy
4 tablespoons rum

Chop the ginger, apricots, raisins and sultanas and combine them in a large bowl with the currants, mixed peel and chopped blanched almonds. Peel, core and grate the apples and mix them in a separate bowl with the orange and lemon rinds and juices. Stir the apple and sugar into the chopped fruit, then grate the carrots and add them to the bowl with the spices, brandy and rum.

Leave the mincemeat to stand for a couple of days, stirring it frequently. Transfer it to clean jars and cover each with an airtight lid. Allow to mature for at least 3 weeks before use.

Honeyed Mincemeat

*This is a chunky mincemeat which makes a pleasant change from
the traditional close-textured recipes.*

Makes about 2.25–2.75 kg/5–6 lb

225 g/8 oz shredded suet
350 g/12 oz raisins
225 g/8 oz sultanas
225 g/8 oz chopped mixed peel
350 g/12 oz currants
100 g/4 oz almonds, chopped
225 g/8 oz clear honey
4 tablespoons lemon juice
150 ml/¼ pint orange juice
150 ml/¼ pint brandy
½ teaspoon ground mixed spice

In a large bowl mix the suet with the raisins, sultanas, chopped
peel and currants. Stir in the almonds. Melt the honey in a pan
with the lemon and orange juice, add the brandy and stir the
liquid into the dried fruit. Sprinkle the spice on top, stir well and
cover the bowl.

Leave the mincemeat to stand for 2 weeks, stirring it every day
until the fruit has absorbed most of the juices. Pack it into clean
jars, pressing the fruit well down into the juices. Cover with
airtight lids and allow to mature for at least 1 month before use.

Chutneys
and Ketchups

HOME-MADE chutney is probably one of the most useful savoury accompaniments to have in the cupboard. It will always cheer up a simple cheese sandwich, but that is only the beginning of the many varied and exciting combinations which can be achieved with this preserve.

In this chapter you will find recipes for chutneys and ketchups ranging from mild, sweet preserves to complement lighter cheeses and poultry, to hot spicy concoctions which can pep up a curry, be used to marinate chicken portions or add a little spice to some plain boiled rice. As long as they are stored in airtight jars or bottles, chutneys should keep well for anything from 9 months to 1 year, and ketchups for about 6 months.

Unlike many commercially prepared chutneys, the flavours of the fruits and vegetables used in your home-made preserve will be easily distinguishable – and you will probably find that you eat far more of it! So be prepared to launch into making further batches of your favourite chutney; or, if you are feeling more adventurous, try another recipe – a ketchup, perhaps, to liven up a salad dressing, spice up a barbecue or add flavour to a simple grilled chop. Why not experiment by adding chutneys and ketchups to meat and poultry casseroles, sauces and dressings, pizzas and pies? In fact, make full use of the concentrated flavours which they can add to your everyday dishes.

Apple Chutney

Make this simple chutney sweet or vinegary, whichever you prefer. The ingredients below give a fairly sweet chutney, so reduce the sugar by 75 g/3 oz for a slightly sharper preserve.

Makes about 2.25 kg/5 lb

1.5 kg/3 lb cooking apples
450 g/1 lb onions
50 g/2 oz raisins
50 g/2 oz fresh root ginger
1 small green pepper
1 tablespoon mustard powder
2 teaspoons ground coriander
3 cloves garlic, crushed
275 g/10 oz demerara sugar
600 ml/1 pint vinegar

Peel, core and chop the apples, chop the onions and raisins and grate the ginger. Remove the stalk, seeds and pith from the pepper and chop the flesh. Mix all these prepared ingredients together in a large saucepan, add the mustard, coriander, garlic and sugar and pour in the vinegar.

Bring the mixture to the boil, stirring occasionally so that all the ingredients are thoroughly combined. Cover the pan, reduce the heat and simmer the chutney for 1 hour. Stir the ingredients frequently during cooking to make sure they do not stick to the pan.

Transfer the chutney to warmed pots and cover immediately with airtight lids. Allow to mature for a few weeks if possible.

Apple and Date Chutney

(Illustrated on page 85)

This is a thick, sweet chutney with a good flavour. It makes an excellent sandwich filling and goes very well with mature cheeses.

Makes about 2.25 g/5 lb

1 kg/2 lb cooking apples
450 g/1 lb onions
450 g/1 lb cooking dates
275 g/10 oz muscovado sugar
1 teaspoon mustard powder
$\frac{1}{2}$ teaspoon ginger
$\frac{1}{2}$ teaspoon turmeric
600 ml/1 pint vinegar

Peel, core and slice the apples, chop the onions and finely chop the dates. Mix these ingredients with the sugar, mustard, ginger and turmeric in a large saucepan and pour in the vinegar. Bring the mixture slowly to the boil, stirring until the sugar has dissolved, cover the pan and reduce the heat. Allow the chutney to simmer for about 40–45 minutes, stirring it frequently during cooking, as it is quite thick and may burn.

Transfer the chutney to warmed jars and cover these immediately with airtight lids. The flavour improves if you leave this chutney to mature for 3–4 weeks.

Rhubarb and Apple Chutney

Dried figs add an unusual flavour to this chutney. The combination of the sharp rhubarb with the sweet figs makes a chutney which is delicious as an accompaniment to cold roast beef or lamb or grilled lamb chops and hamburgers.

Makes 1.5–1.75 kg/3–4 lb

450 g/1 lb trimmed rhubarb
450 g/1 lb cooking apples
225 g/8 oz onions
350 g/12 oz dark soft brown sugar
1 teaspoon ground ginger
1 teaspoon ground mixed spice
225 g/8 oz dried figs
450 ml/¾ pint vinegar

Slice the rhubarb into a large saucepan. Peel, core and slice the apples and put them in the pan. Finely chop the onions and add them to the prepared fruit, together with the sugar and spices. Chop the figs and stir them into the ingredients with the vinegar. Bring the chutney to the boil, cover the pan and reduce the heat.

Simmer the chutney for 1 hour, then uncover the pan and allow any excess moisture to evaporate by simmering the mixture rapidly for about 30 minutes. Stir the chutney occasionally while it is cooking to prevent it sticking to the pan.

Transfer the chutney to warmed pots and cover these with airtight lids. As with most chutneys and pickles, the flavour will mature if you store it for a few weeks.

Red Tomato Chutney

Home-grown tomatoes give the best flavour; but try making this chutney, too, with tomatoes you can often buy quite cheaply on market stalls.

Makes about 1.5–1.75 kg/3–4 lb

1 kg/2 lb ripe tomatoes
225 g/8 oz sultanas
450 g/1 lb onions
175 g/6 oz muscovado sugar
1½ teaspoons ground coriander
1½ teaspoons ground ginger
2 cloves garlic, crushed
175 ml/6 fl oz vinegar

Place the tomatoes in a large bowl, cover them with boiling water and allow them to stand for 30 seconds. Then drain, peel and chop them, together with the sultanas. Finely chop the onions. Mix all the ingredients in a large saucepan and bring them to the boil, stirring continuously. Cover the pan, reduce the heat and simmer the chutney for 1¼ hours, stirring occasionally to make sure it does not stick to the pan. Uncover the pan and continue to cook for a further 15 minutes.

Transfer the chutney to warmed jars and cover these immediately with airtight lids. Allow to mature for 1 month before serving.

Green Tomato Chutney

If you grow your own tomatoes you will almost certainly be left with a few pounds of unripened fruit at the end of the season. Even if you store them carefully and allow them to ripen indoors, they will never be very successful as their skins will always remain tough. So chop up your green tomatoes and make a tempting chutney out of them – you will find it far more satisfying to eat than a few tough old red ones.

Makes about 1.75 kg/4 lb

1 kg/2 lb green tomatoes
450 g/1 lb onions
450 g/1 lb cooking apples
2 green chillies
2 cloves garlic, crushed
1 teaspoon ground ginger
generous pinch of ground cloves
generous pinch of turmeric
50 g/2 oz raisins
225 g/8 oz dark soft brown sugar
300 ml/½ pint vinegar

Finely chop the tomatoes and onions. Peel, core and chop the apples and chop the chillies. Mix all these ingredients together in a large saucepan and add the garlic, ginger, cloves and turmeric. Stir in the raisins, sugar and vinegar and bring the chutney to the boil.

Cover the pan and reduce the heat, then simmer the chutney for about 1¼ – 1½ hours or until it has thickened. Stir it frequently during cooking to prevent it from sticking to the pan. Pour it into warmed pots and cover them with airtight lids. Leave the chutney to mature for a few weeks.

Tomato and Apple Chutney

Simple and sweet, this chutney is a favourite ingredient in sandwiches made with mature Cheddar cheese or cold cooked meats. Add your favourite herbs and spices to vary the flavour: garlic, fresh root ginger, curry powder or any of the curry spices – cardamom, coriander, cinnamon, cumin – can all be added in small quantities.

Makes about 1.75 kg/4 lb

1 kg/2 lb ripe tomatoes
1 kg/2 lb cooking apples
2 large onions
100 g/4 oz raisins
225 g/8 oz soft dark brown sugar
1 teaspoon turmeric
1 teaspoon salt
freshly ground black pepper
450 ml/$\frac{3}{4}$ pint vinegar

Place the tomatoes in a large bowl, cover them with boiling water and leave them for about 30 seconds. Drain and peel them. Peel, core and chop the apples, chop the tomatoes and onions and stir all these ingredients together in a large saucepan. Roughly chop the raisins and add them to the pan together with the sugar, turmeric and salt. Season generously with pepper and pour in the vinegar.

  Bring the mixture to the boil, stirring frequently, and simmer it uncovered for about 2 hours. Stir the chutney from time to time to make sure it does not stick to the pan. Transfer it to warmed pots and cover these immediately with airtight lids. This chutney is best if allowed to mature for 1 month.

Blackberry and Apple Chutney

Blackberries are so plentiful in the autumn that it seems a shame not to take advantage of one of the few free fruits that we can all really enjoy.
Try making this savoury chutney instead of your usual bramble jelly. I am sure you will find it delicious with the richer roast meats like pork and lamb.

Makes about 1.75 kg/4 lb

1 kg/2 lb blackberries
1 kg/2 lb cooking apples
2 large onions
1 teaspoon salt
2 tablespoons grated fresh root ginger
2 cloves garlic, crushed
100 g/4 oz dried apricots
225 g/8 oz demerara sugar
300 ml/½ pint Spiced Vinegar (page 98)

Lightly wash and drain the blackberries. Peel, core and slice the apples and chop the onions. Mix all these ingredients together in a large saucepan and add the salt, ginger and garlic. Chop the apricots and add them to the pan with the sugar and vinegar. Stir well to combine all the ingredients.

Bring the chutney to the boil, cover the pan and reduce the heat. Simmer for about 1 hour, stirring occasionally to prevent the mixture sticking to the bottom of the pan. At the end of the cooking time the chutney should be thickened. If there is still a lot of moisture, remove the lid and boil the chutney for a few minutes to allow the excess to evaporate.

Transfer the chutney to warmed pots and cover them immediately with airtight lids. Allow it to mature for at least 3 weeks.

Plum and Pear Chutney

Combine the tangy flavour of plums with the delicate pears to make a delicious chutney for serving with most cold roast meats, particularly pork, and the stronger mature Cheddars.

Makes about 1.75 kg/4 lb

1 kg/2 lb cooking pears
1 kg/2 lb cooking plums
450 g/1 lb onions, chopped
300 ml/$\frac{1}{2}$ pint Orange Vinegar (page 97) or
Spiced Vinegar (page 98)
2 cloves garlic, crushed
2 tablespoons grated fresh root ginger
225 g/8 oz cooking dates
225 g/8 oz dark soft brown sugar

Peel, halve and core the pears. Slice and place them in a large saucepan. Halve and stone the plums and add them to the pan followed by the chopped onion and the vinegar. Add the garlic and ginger and stir well. Chop the dates and stir them into the mixture together with the sugar.

Bring the chutney to the boil, cover the pan and reduce the heat, then simmer it for 1$\frac{1}{2}$ hours. Stir it occasionally during cooking to prevent it from sticking to the bottom of the pan.

Transfer the chutney to hot pots and cover these immediately with airtight lids. Allow it to mature for at least 2 weeks.

Banana Chutney

Economical to prepare, mild but well-flavoured, this chutney should be served with hot curries, spiced meats and matured or smoked cheeses.

Makes about 1.5−1.75 kg/3−4 lb

1 kg/2 lb bananas
450 g/1 lb onions
1 large green pepper
175 g/6 oz raisins
225 g/8 oz dark soft brown sugar
$\frac{1}{4}$ teaspoon ground mixed spice
$\frac{1}{2}$ teaspoon paprika
450 ml/$\frac{3}{4}$ pint vinegar

Slice the bananas, chop the onions and mix them together in a large saucepan. Remove the seeds and pith from the pepper and roughly chop it, then add it to the pan with the raisins, sugar, spices and vinegar.

Bring the mixture to the boil, stirring continuously, reduce the heat, cover the pan and simmer the chutney for about $1\frac{1}{2}$−$1\frac{3}{4}$ hours. Remember to stir it from time to time to make sure it does not stick to the pan. Remove the lid and simmer the chutney for a further 15 minutes, then pot it in warmed jars and cover these with airtight lids. Allow the chutney to mature for 2 weeks.

Tangy Fruit Chutney

Chopped pared orange rind adds a special touch to this simple fruit chutney. For a more pronounced orange flavour, the rind of two oranges may be used.
Serve it with mature Cheddar cheese and cooked meats.

Makes about 1.5 kg/3 lb

575 g/1¼ lb cooking apples
450 g/1 lb onions
100 g/4 oz cooking dates
175 g/6 oz raisins
thinly pared rind and juice of 1 orange
225 g/8 oz light soft brown sugar
½ teaspoon turmeric
300 ml/½ pint vinegar

Peel, core and slice the apples. Finely chop the onions, dates, raisins and orange rind. Mix all these ingredients in a large saucepan and pour in the orange juice. Add the sugar, turmeric and vinegar and bring the chutney to the boil, stirring frequently to mix all the ingredients.

Reduce the heat, cover the pan and allow the chutney to simmer for 1 hour, stirring oecasionally to keep it from sticking to the pan. Remove the lid and continue cooking it for a further 15 minutes until it has thickened. Pot it in warmed jars and cover these immediately with airtight lids. Store the chutney for at least 1 week to allow it to mature.

Clockwise from the top: *Mixed Vegetable Pickle (page 108); Apple and Date Chutney (page 76); Apricot Chutney (page 88); Pickled Onions (page 98).*

Pear and Gooseberry Chutney

The bland pears mix well with the tart gooseberries to give a chutney which can be served with mackerel, both smoked and unsmoked, frankfurters and smoked sausages and cheeses.

Makes about 1.5 kg/3 lb

1 kg/2 lb cooking pears
1 kg/2 lb cooking gooseberries
2 large onions
25 g/1 oz fresh root ginger
50 g/2 oz sultanas
1 teaspoon turmeric
2 teaspoons salt
175 g/6 oz sugar
300 ml/½ pint vinegar

Peel, core and chop the pears. Top and tail the gooseberries and finely chop the onions and ginger. Roughly chop the sultanas and mix all these prepared ingredients in a large saucepan. Add the turmeric and salt, sugar and vinegar, stirring well to mix the ingredients.

Bring the chutney to the boil, reduce the heat and simmer it, uncovered, for 1 hour or until the fruit is pulpy and the chutney thickened. Remember to stir the mixture frequently during cooking to prevent it from sticking to the base of the pan.

Transfer the chutney to warmed jars and cover these with airtight lids. Leave it to mature for 3–4 weeks.

Clockwise from the top: Pickled Peaches (page 106); Red Pepper Pickle (page 111); Pickled Cabbage (page 99); Courgette Pickle (page 114); Brazil Nut and Apricot Pickle (page 118).

Apricot Chutney

(Illustrated on page 85)

This is a delicious, fruity chutney, ideal for serving with roast pork, lamb and duck. It also makes a good side dish with hot curries and highly spiced dishes.

Makes about 1.5 kg/3 lb

450 g/1 lb dried apricots
450 g/1 lb onions
2 cloves garlic, crushed
$\frac{1}{2}$ teaspoon turmeric
1 teaspoon mustard powder
225 g/8 oz sugar
600 ml/1 pint cider vinegar

Chop the apricots and onions and mix them together in a saucepan. Add all the remaining ingredients and stir well, then allow the mixture to stand for 2 hours.

Heat the chutney gently, stirring continuously until the sugar has dissolved, bring it to the boil and reduce the heat. Cover the pan and simmer the chutney for about 2 hours, stirring occasionally to make sure it does not stick to the pan. The fruit should be thoroughly softened and the chutney thickened.

Transfer it to warmed pots and cover these immediately with airtight lids.

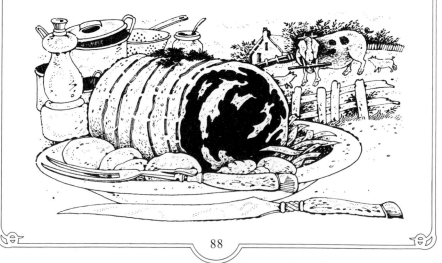

Peach Chutney

(Illustrated on page 103)

The delicate flavour of the peaches makes this a good accompaniment with ripe, creamy Brie cheese, full fat soft cheeses and roast poultry. Try to save a pot specially for serving with your cold roast Christmas turkey.

Makes about 1.5–1.75 kg/3–4 lb

12 peaches
450 g/1 lb onions
2 cloves garlic, crushed
2 tablespoons grated fresh root ginger
100 g/4 oz cooking dates
225 g/8 oz demerara sugar
300 ml/½ pint Orange Vinegar (page 97) or
red wine vinegar
salt and pepper

Place the peaches in a large bowl and cover them with boiling water. Leave them to stand for about 1 minute, then drain and peel them. Halve and stone the fruit and cut it into thick slices.

Chop the onions and place them in a saucepan with the peaches, garlic and ginger. Chop the dates and add them to the pan with the sugar and vinegar. Add a generous sprinkling of salt and pepper and bring the mixture to the boil, stirring until the sugar has dissolved.

Cover the pan, reduce the heat and simmer the chutney for about 45 minutes, until thickened. Stir it frequently during cooking to prevent it from sticking to the pan.

Transfer the chutney to warmed pots and cover each pot immediately with an airtight lid. Label the chutney and store it for 2 weeks to allow the flavour to mature.

Herb Chutney

Here is one way to preserve the unique flavour of fresh herbs. You can make a mint chutney to serve with lamb, a rosemary and sage chutney for pork or a mixed herb chutney to add to casseroles and supper dishes. You will find that these chutneys also taste very good with full fat soft cheese or creamy cheeses such as Brie and Camembert.

Makes about 1.75 kg/4 lb

1.5 kg/3 lb cooking apples
1 kg/2 lb onions
225 g/8 oz dried apricots
225 g/8 oz raisins
2 tablespoons grated fresh root ginger
350 g/12 oz sugar
450 ml/$\frac{3}{4}$ pint white vinegar
100 g/4 oz fresh mint *or* 50 g/2 oz mixed fresh
rosemary and sage *or* 100 g/4 oz mixed fresh herbs including
parsley, mint, thyme, a little rosemary and a little sage

Peel, core and slice the apples. Finely chop the onions and apricots and roughly chop the raisins. Mix all these prepared ingredients together in a large saucepan and add the ginger, sugar and vinegar.

Bring the mixture to the boil, cover the pan and simmer the chutney over a low heat for about 45–60 minutes, stirring occasionally, until the apples are reduced to a pulp and the preserve has thickened.

Meanwhile, take all the leaves off the chosen herbs and chop them finely, discarding the stalks. Add the chopped herbs to the chutney at the end of the cooking time, stir well and bring it once more to the boil. Pour the chutney into hot pots and cover them immediately with airtight lids.

Chilli Chutney

*This spicy chutney is very hot indeed – be warned and do not
delve into the pot with a large spoon. Rather, take a teaspoonful
with your curry and allow only the merest hint of it to add a
special, spicy flavour to each forkful.*
*As well as being an excellent accompaniment to curries, small
quantities of this chutney will spice up an otherwise plain meal.
Or mix a little of it with natural yogurt, spread the mixture over
meat or poultry before cooking and you have an exciting, highly
seasoned marinade.*

Makes 675–900 g / 1½–2 lb

450 g / 1 lb fresh chillies, red or green
6 cloves garlic, crushed
4 tablespoons ground cumin
2 tablespoons turmeric
1 large onion, finely chopped
1 tablespoon salt
25 g / 1 oz fresh root ginger, grated
300 ml / ½ pint oil
3 tablespoons muscovado sugar
300 ml / ½ pint vinegar

Remove the stalks from the chillies and chop the chillies very
finely, seeds and all. The chopping process is easy if you have a
food processor, but a good sharp knife is quite adequate. In fact,
I use a large Chinese meat cleaver which chops the chillies in no
time at all.

Mix the chillies, garlic, cumin, turmeric, chopped onion, salt,
ginger and oil in a saucepan and fry the ingredients together for
15 minutes. Stir the mixture frequently to prevent it from
sticking to the pan. Add the sugar and vinegar and bring the
mixture to the boil. Cover the pan and boil the chutney for 10
minutes, stirring occasionally to make sure it does not stick.

Transfer it immediately to hot jars and cover these with
airtight lids. Stir the chutney well before use as the oil will
separate out on standing.

Simple Tomato Ketchup

Home-made ketchups are very different from the commercial product. They are spiced fruit or vegetable purées which can be delicate or pronounced in flavour; they make ideal condiments for roast or grilled meats and they can be added to sauces and mayonnaise-based salad dressings.
Here is the classic ketchup, to be served with grills, hamburgers or as a dip for meat fondues.

Makes about 1.15 litres/2 pints

1.5 kg/3 lb ripe tomatoes (preferably home-grown for a good flavour)
450 g/1 lb onions
175 g/6 oz sugar
3 tablespoons mustard powder
3 cloves garlic, crushed
1 teaspoon salt
150 ml/¼ pint red wine vinegar

Roughly chop the tomatoes and onions and mix them in a saucepan with all the other ingredients. Bring the mixture to the boil and simmer it, stirring occasionally, for 45 minutes. Do not cover the pan.

  Allow the ketchup to cool slightly, then blend it to a purée in a liquidiser. Press the purée through a sieve and return it to the rinsed-out saucepan. Bring it once more to the boil. Take the pan off the heat, pour the ketchup into warmed bottles and cover these immediately with airtight lids.

Tomato and Apple Ketchup

This fruity ketchup will liven up grilled chops, steaks, hamburgers and sausages. You can also add it to the juices left in the pan from fried meats and warm it through to make a spicy sauce.

Makes about 600–900 ml/1–1½ pints

350 g/12 oz cooking apples
1.25 kg/2½ lb tomatoes
225 g/8 oz onions
175 g/6 oz demerara sugar
2 large cloves garlic, peeled
1 teaspoon paprika
2 teaspoons dried marjoram
450 ml/¾ pint Spiced Vinegar (page 98)

Wash the apples and remove the stalks. Roughly chop them, peel, core and all, and place them in a large saucepan. Wash the tomatoes and onions but do not peel either of them. Chop and add them to the pan. Sprinkle in the sugar followed by all the remaining ingredients and bring the mixture slowly to the boil, stirring continuously. Cover the pan and boil the ketchup steadily for about 1 hour, stirring from time to time to make sure it does not stick to the pan. You may have to reduce the heat slightly towards the end of cooking time to prevent the mixture from boiling too hard.

   Allow to cool slightly, then purée the ketchup in a liquidiser before pressing it through a fine sieve to remove any pips and trimmings. Return it to the pan, bring it once more to the boil and pour it into warmed bottles or jars. Cover each immediately with an airtight lid.

Mushroom Ketchup

This is a simple recipe which produces a well-flavoured ketchup,
useful as a seasoning for casseroles, meat loaves and meat pies and
dark, rich sauces and gravies. Don't be put off by its
unusual colour!
You can also add mushroom ketchup to salad dressings, but take
care here as it could discolour them.

Makes 600 ml/1 pint

350 g/12 oz large, open mushrooms
300 ml/$\frac{1}{2}$ pint vinegar
1 tablespoon salt
100 g/4 oz dark soft brown sugar
freshly ground black pepper

Cut the mushrooms into quarters and place them in a saucepan.
Add all the other ingredients, season generously with black
pepper and bring the mixture to the boil, stirring frequently to
mix in and shrink the mushrooms. Cover the pan, reduce the
heat and simmer the mushrooms, stirring from time to time, for
30–40 minutes.

Allow the ketchup to cool slightly before blending it to a purée
in a liquidiser. Return the purée to the rinsed saucepan and bring
it back to boiling point. Pour it into warmed bottles and cover
these immediately with airtight tops.

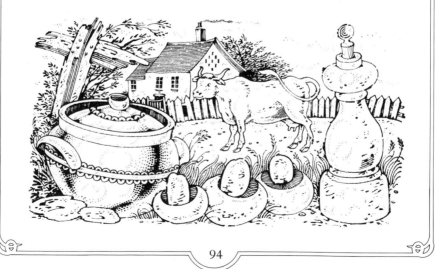

Hot Apple Ketchup

Take care when using this ketchup as it is quite hot. Eat it in small quantities or use it to add a little life to slightly bland meat dishes.
Hot Apple Ketchup also makes an excellent marinade when spread on meat or fish a short while before cooking.

Makes about 1.15 litres/2 pints

1 kg/2 lb cooking apples
450 g/1 lb onions
4 green chillies
6 cloves garlic
10 whole green cardamoms
2 teaspoons ground ginger
2 teaspoons mustard seeds
600 ml/1 pint vinegar
175 g/6 oz sugar

Wash the apples and onions and chop them roughly, without removing the peel. Chop the chillies. Place these ingredients in a large saucepan and add the garlic, spices, vinegar and sugar. Bring the mixture to the boil, cover the pan and simmer it for 45 minutes, stirring occasionally to make sure it does not stick to the pan. Allow the mixture to cool slightly, then press it through a fine sieve and return the purée to the rinsed-out pan.

Bring the ketchup once more to the boil and pour it into warmed bottles. Cover immediately with airtight lids.

Pickles
and Relishes

IF YOUR taste for pickles has never extended further than
pickled onions, here is your chance to experiment and
discover the exciting range open to you – home-pickled onions
and cabbage for Boxing Day supper, spiced eggs and piccalilli
for Bonfire Night and cucumber, red pepper or mixed
vegetable pickle for a summer barbecue.

Among the recipes in this chapter you will find a selection of
pickled fruits, vegetables and other foods which are simply
prepared by preserving the ingredients in vinegar. Perhaps one
of the easiest pickles to prepare is pickled eggs – they are
certainly easily consumed in our house! I have also included a
selection of recipes for pickles which have thick sauces, but in
which you can still identify the fruits and vegetables. This is the
difference between a chutney and a pickle – in the former the
ingredients are finely chopped and cooked to a pulp, whereas a
good pickle should be chunky.

If you are a lover of curries and spicy foods you will find a few
recipes which should provide you with a variety of accompaniments for such dishes – Aubergine Pickle is mild and spicy,
Coconut Pickle is crunchy and sweet and Hot Lime Pickle is for
the hardened curry-eaters only!

If your palate is accustomed to the more traditional foods – to
roasts and grills, boiled meats and cold pies – you too will find
just the accompaniment in one, or many, of the relishes.
Tangy or sweet, lightly or markedly spiced, they will do justice
to any cold roast or simple boiled ham.

Flavoured Vinegars

Vinegars flavoured with fruits or herbs are excellent for making salad dressings and sauces. They may also be used for pickling onions, eggs, new potatoes and fruits, such as plums and apples.

Wine vinegar is best for flavouring, but white and cider vinegars may also be used.

Herb Vinegars

Mint, tarragon, rosemary, thyme, basil, lemon balm, marjoram, sage and chives are all suitable for flavouring vinegar. If you mix herbs, however, balance the more delicately flavoured ones with the stronger. For example, use thyme and rosemary, both herbs with very marked flavours, in smaller quantities than lemon balm or marjoram.

Take 175 g/6 oz of your chosen fresh herb or herbs. Wash and dry them and place them in a large saucepan. Pour in 1.15 litres/ 2 pints wine vinegar and heat the mixture slowly to boiling point. Transfer it to a large bowl, mashing the herbs well with a wooden spoon. Cover the bowl and leave the vinegar to stand for about 2–3 weeks, stirring it each day. Strain it through a fine sieve into bottles. Add small sprigs of the appropriate herb to each and cover with screw tops.

Orange and Lemon Vinegars

Use 6 oranges or lemons for every 1.15 litres/2 pints wine vinegar.

Pare the rind from the fruit, chop it finely and place it in a large saucepan. Squeeze in the fruit juice and pour in the vinegar. Heat the mixture slowly to boiling point, then transfer it to a large bowl. Cover and leave the vinegar to stand for 2 weeks. Strain it through a fine sieve and pour it into bottles. Add a thinly pared strip of orange or lemon rind to each bottle and cover with screw tops.

Garlic Vinegar

Allow 2 bulbs of garlic for each 1.15 litres/2 pints vinegar.

Peel and chop the garlic cloves and place them in a large saucepan with the vinegar. Bring the mixture slowly to the boil, then pour it into a large bowl and allow it to stand, covered, for 1 week. Strain it through a fine sieve into screw-topped bottles.

Spiced Vinegar

2.25 litres/4 pints vinegar
1 cinnamon stick
12 cloves
2 tablespoons coriander seeds
1 tablespoon mustard seeds
4 dried red chillies
2 teaspoons whole black peppercorns

Mix the vinegar in a saucepan with all the spices and heat gently to boiling point. Reduce the heat, cover the pan and simmer the mixture gently for 15 minutes. Leave it to cool. Strain the cooled vinegar through a fine sieve, bottle it and use it as required.

Pickled Onions

(Illustrated on page 85)

Remember to prepare these at the end of November so that they are ready to serve with your cold Christmas turkey.

1.5 kg/3 lb pickling onions, peeled
about 50 g/2 oz salt
900 ml–1.15 litres/1½–2 pints Spiced Vinegar (above),
made with white vinegar

Place the onions in a large bowl and sprinkle them with the salt, tossing them well to make sure they are completely coated. Allow the onions to stand overnight, then quickly rinse and dry them. Pack them into large, wide-necked jars and pour over the vinegar, shaking the jars lightly to make sure that the vinegar runs down between the onions and covers them completely.

Allow the onions to mature for at least 2 weeks before eating them – they are best after 1 month and will keep for 6 months.

Pickled Eggs

I find these eggs a useful store cupboard item as they are quickly prepared and will turn a few salad ingredients into a light meal. Served with cheese and warm, fresh bread they are quite delicious – in fact they probably won't stay in the cupboard for long!

6 small eggs
900 ml/1½ pints Spiced Vinegar (opposite), preferably made with white vinegar

Hard boil the eggs, plunge them straight into cold water and shell them. Place them in a wide-necked jar and pour in the vinegar, making sure that it runs down between the eggs and covers them completely. Put the lid on the jar and allow the eggs to stand for 1 week before eating them. They may be stored for up to 3 months.

Pickled Cabbage

(Illustrated on page 86)

As well as tasting delicious with cold meats and cheeses, pickled cabbage can be used as an ingredient in salads and side dishes.

1 medium red cabbage (about 1 kg/2 lb)
about 50 g/2 oz salt
about 1.4 litres/2½ pints Spiced Vinegar (opposite),
preferably made with white vinegar

Discard any damaged outer leaves from the cabbage and shred the rest finely, removing the hard central core. Layer the cabbage in a large bowl, sprinkling it with the salt, and leave it overnight. Lightly rinse and thoroughly dry the cabbage, then pack it into wide-necked jars. Do not pack it too firmly or the vinegar will not reach all the shreds. Carefully pour in the vinegar, allowing time for it to run down between the pieces of cabbage and to cover it completely. Cover the jars and allow the cabbage to stand for 1 week. It will store for 3 months.

Pickled Red Peppers

(Illustrated on page 103)

These vegetables are useful ingredients in salads, pizzas and sauces. You can also add them to well-flavoured casseroles, but be careful not to make the result vinegary.

4 red peppers
about 600 ml/1 pint white vinegar
225 g/8 oz sugar
1 tablespoon salt

Cut the tops off the peppers and scoop out all the pith and seeds. Blanch them in boiling water for about 3 minutes or until they are just soft. Dry them well on absorbent kitchen paper.

Pour the vinegar into a saucepan, add the sugar and salt and bring the mixture to the boil. Cover the pan and simmer for 10 minutes. Pack the peppers into large jars and pour the boiling vinegar over them. Cover the jars with airtight lids and leave the peppers to mature for 1 week. Eat them within 6 months.

Pickled Beetroot

Serve sliced pickled beetroot with cold meats or thoroughly drain it, mix it with a little mayonnaise and serve it as a salad.

1 kg/2 lb beetroot, freshly cooked
1 onion, finely chopped
about 900 ml/1½ pints Orange or Spiced Vinegar
(pages 97 and 98)

Peel and thickly slice the hot beetroot. Layer the beetroot and chopped onion in a large wide-necked jar with an airtight lid.

Heat the vinegar to boiling point and pour it slowly into the jar, allowing it to run in between the slices of beetroot. Make sure that the beetroot is completely covered with the vinegar. Top the jar immediately with an airtight lid and allow it to stand for 2 weeks. Pickled beetroot can be stored for 4–6 months.

Spiced Eggs

(Illustrated on page 103)

The spices used in this recipe give the eggs a mild curry flavour which is delicious when combined with a little mayonnaise. They are a great stand-by for a quick starter and add interest to most curries and cold meat dishes.

900 ml/1½ pints white vinegar
1 dried red chilli
6 whole green cardamoms
2 tablespoons coriander seeds
5 cloves
½ teaspoon turmeric
4 cloves garlic
½ teaspoon salt
1 small onion
6 small eggs

Mix the vinegar in a saucepan with the chilli, all the spices, the garlic and salt and heat the mixture gently to boiling point. Cover the pan and simmer for 5 minutes, then leave the vinegar to cool and strain it through a fine sieve.

Slice the onion into thin rings. Hard boil the eggs and plunge them immediately into cold water. Shell them and place them in a large, wide-necked jar with the onion rings. Carefully pour the spiced vinegar into the jar, ensuring that it runs right down between the eggs and covers them completely. Put the lid on the jar and allow it to stand for 1 week. The eggs may be stored for up to 3 months.

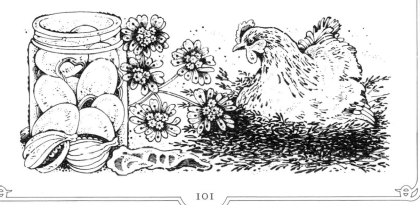

Pickled Mushrooms

Occasionally it is possible to buy perfect little mushrooms quite cheaply, either from a good market stall, or a greengrocer or a mushroom farm. Add the herb of your choice to the mushroom jar; one or two small sprigs will be enough to flavour them.
Slice the mushrooms for use in salads or in pizza fillings, alternatively simply serve them on cocktail sticks with cubes of cheese or cooked ham.

450 g/1 lb small button mushrooms
about 600 ml/1 pint white vinegar
sprig of rosemary, thyme, sage or basil

Wipe and trim the mushrooms and pack about three-quarters of them into a large jar. Pour in enough vinegar to cover them and add the herb. Cover the jar and allow the mushrooms to stand overnight.

Next day you will find that they have shrunk; they usually shrink to their full extent overnight or after about 24 hours. Pack the remaining mushrooms into the jar, making sure that they are covered in vinegar before storing them.

Pickled mushrooms should be kept for at least 1 week before being eaten. They may be stored for up to 3 months.

From the top: *Peach Chutney (page 89); Pickled Red Peppers (page 100);*
Spiced Eggs (page 101); Hot Lime Pickle (page 121); Mango Pickle (page 116);
Coconut Pickle (page 120).

Pickled Cucumbers

Pickled cucumbers are served with cold roast and boiled meats, hamburgers and barbecued foods or with meat salads and continental sausages. The sugar is an optional ingredient in this recipe – add it if you like sweeter pickles.

450 g/1 lb ridge cucumbers (about 6)
1 medium onion
about 25 g/1 oz salt
450–600 ml/¾–1 pint Spiced Vinegar (page 98)
50 g/2 oz sugar (optional)
small bunch of fresh dill

Wash and trim the cucumbers and dry them thoroughly. Put them into a large bowl. Chop the onion fairly finely and scatter it over the cucumbers. Sprinkle the vegetables generously with salt, shaking the bowl so that they are completely coated. Cover the bowl and leave to stand overnight.

Heat the vinegar in a pan with the sugar, if used, stirring until the sugar has dissolved. Bring the mixture to the boil. Rinse and dry the cucumbers and onion and pack them loosely into jars. Divide the dill between the jars and pour in the hot vinegar. Cover immediately with airtight lids and allow the pickled cucumbers to stand for at least 2 weeks. They can be stored for up to 3 months.

Clockwise from the top: *hamburger with Redcurrant Relish (page 126)*;
Beetroot Relish (page 122); Sweet Corn Relish (page 123); Piccalilli (page 109); Tomato and Onion Relish (page 124).

Pickled Peaches

(Illustrated on page 86)

These are simple to prepare and taste absolutely delicious with cold roast meats, boiled or baked ham and platters of mixed cold meats, such as salami, garlic sausage, ham sausage and brawn.

900 ml/1½ pints Orange Vinegar (page 97)
450 g/1 lb sugar
2 cinnamon sticks
10 cloves
4 cardamoms
1 clove garlic, crushed
8–10 ripe peaches

Pour the vinegar into a large saucepan and add the sugar. Stir in the spices and garlic and heat slowly to boiling point, stirring continuously until the sugar has dissolved. Bring to the boil and cover the pan, then reduce the heat and simmer the vinegar for 30 minutes. Take the pan off the heat and allow it to cool. Strain the cold vinegar through a fine sieve and return it to the rinsed-out saucepan. Reheat it to boiling point.

Meanwhile, place the peaches in a large bowl and cover them with boiling water. Leave them to stand for 1 minute, then drain and peel them. Carefully halve the fruit and remove the stones.

Pack the peaches loosely into wide-necked jars and pour in the boiling vinegar. Cover immediately with airtight lids and keep them for 2 weeks before use. They may be stored for 3–4 months.

Pickled Apricots

Similar to pickled peaches, these fruits are the perfect accompaniments to roast and cold meats. They are also ideal for serving on cocktail sticks with cubes of Cheddar, Gruyère or smoked cheese, cooked ham or slices of frankfurter.

900 ml/1½ pints wine vinegar, white vinegar or cider vinegar
225 g/8 oz sugar
4 tablespoons pickling spice
2 cinnamon sticks
1 large onion, chopped
1 teaspoon salt
450 g/1 lb apricots

Pour the vinegar into a large saucepan and add the sugar, spices, onion and salt. Stir the mixture until the sugar has dissolved, then bring it to the boil, cover the pan and reduce the heat. Simmer the vinegar for 40 minutes, take it off the heat and allow it to cool. Strain the vinegar through a fine sieve and return it to the rinsed-out saucepan.

Pack the fruit loosely into wide-necked heatproof jars. Bring the vinegar to the boil and pour it over the fruit. Cover the jars with airtight lids and allow the apricots to stand for 2 weeks before use. They may be kept for 3–4 months.

Variation

Cooking pears may be substituted for the apricots. Peel, halve and core them, pack them into jars and proceed as above. Allow the pears to mature and soften for at least 3 weeks before use.

Mixed Vegetable Pickle

(Illustrated on page 85)

*This is a rich, dark pickle which can be made with almost any
vegetables; French beans or sliced runner beans, sweet corn or
broad beans can all be added to the ingredients.
For a tart pickle, use half the quantity of sugar; if you like hot
condiments, add a few finely chopped green chillies.*

Makes about 1.75 kg/4 lb

1 small cauliflower
450 g/1 lb swede
100 g/4 oz carrots
450 g/1 lb cooking apples
100 g/4 oz cooking dates
2 large onions
225 g/8 oz dark soft brown sugar
2 tablespoons mustard powder
2 cloves garlic, crushed
1 tablespoon paprika
1 teaspoon salt
450 ml/$\frac{3}{4}$ pint vinegar

Cut away the outer leaves of the cauliflower and break it into
florets, discarding the hard, main stalk. Peel the swede and
carrots and dice them coarsely. Peel, core and slice the apples.
Chop the dates and onions. Mix all these prepared ingredients in
a large saucepan and add all the remaining ingredients.

Heat the pickle gently, stirring until all the sugar has dissolved,
then bring it to the boil. Cover the pan, reduce the heat and
simmer it for about 1 hour, stirring occasionally. Remove the lid
and continue to cook the pickle at a steady simmer for a further
15 minutes, or until it has thickened.

Transfer it to warmed pots and cover these immediately with
airtight lids. Allow the pickle to mature for 1 month. It will
keep for 6–9 months.

Piccalilli

(Illustrated on page 104)

This pickle is traditionally very spicy with a crunchy texture. Celery and French beans may also be added to the ingredients given below.

Makes about 1 kg/2 lb

1 small cauliflower
½ cucumber
2 onions
2 large carrots
about 50 g/2 oz salt
2 tablespoons plain flour
300 ml/½ pint cider vinegar
225 g/8 oz sugar
½ teaspoon turmeric
½ teaspoon ground ginger
2 teaspoons mustard powder
freshly ground black pepper

Trim the outer leaves from the cauliflower and break it into small florets, discarding any large stalks. Thinly peel and roughly chop the cucumber. Chop the onions and cut the carrots into medium chunks. Place all the prepared vegetables in layers in a large bowl, sprinkling each layer with salt, and leave them to stand overnight. Lightly rinse and thoroughly dry them.

Mix the flour to a smooth cream with a little of the vinegar. Heat the remaining vinegar in a large saucepan with the sugar, spices and mustard, stirring until the sugar has dissolved. Bring to the boil, season the mixture generously with pepper and add the vegetables. Return it to the boil, then reduce the heat and simmer, uncovered, for 10 minutes.

Remove the pan from the heat and gradually stir in the flour mixture. Return it to the heat, bring the pickle to the boil and cook it gently for a further 5 minutes. Transfer it to warmed jars and cover immediately with airtight lids. Piccalilli is ready to eat as soon as it is made and it can be stored for 6–9 months.

Marrow and Onion Pickle

This is a chunky, sweet pickle which tastes good with boiled or baked ham, roast meats and continental sausages.

Makes about 2.75 kg/6 lb

1 medium marrow (about 1.75 kg/4 lb in weight)
1 kg/2 lb small pickling onions
salt
1 green or red pepper
225 g/8 oz cooking dates
1 tablespoon finely grated fresh root ginger
600 ml/1 pint Spiced Vinegar (page 98)
450 g/1 lb demerara sugar

Peel the marrow and cut it in half lengthways. Remove the seeds and cut the flesh into chunks. Peel and halve the onions. Layer the marrow and onions in a large bowl with a liberal sprinkling of salt between each layer, cover and leave the vegetables to stand overnight. Next day rinse and thoroughly dry them.

Place the salted vegetables in a large saucepan. Trim the pepper, remove the seeds and pith and chop the flesh finely, together with the dates. Add these ingredients to the pan with the ginger, vinegar and sugar. Bring the mixture to the boil, stirring well to mix the ingredients. Cover the pan, reduce the heat and simmer the pickle for $1\frac{1}{2}$ hours, until the mixture has thickened. Remember to stir it frequently during cooking to prevent it sticking to the pan.

Transfer the pickle to warmed pots and cover each immediately with an airtight lid. Leave it to mature for 2 weeks. It can be stored for about 6 months.

Red Pepper Pickle

(Illustrated on page 86)

Red and green peppers give a strong, excellent flavour to chutneys and pickles. The combination of dates and peppers in this pickle makes it the perfect accompaniment to mild cheeses, plain pizzas and simple cold pies.

Makes about 1.5 kg/3 lb

3 large red peppers
450 g/1 lb cooking apples
450 g/1 lb onions
225 g/8 oz cooking dates
225 g/8 oz dark soft brown sugar
300 ml/$\frac{1}{2}$ pint vinegar
$\frac{1}{2}$ teaspoon salt

Halve the peppers, remove the seeds, pith and stalks and chop the flesh. Peel, core and slice the cooking apples and chop the onions and dates. Mix all the ingredients in a large saucepan and bring the pickle slowly to the boil.

Reduce the heat, cover the pan and cook the pickle for 1 hour, stirring occasionally, then remove the lid and continue to simmer it for about 45 minutes. By this time, most of the excess moisture should have evaporated to leave a thickened pickle. Pour it into warmed pots and cover each with an airtight lid. Allow the pickle to mature for at least 2 weeks; it will keep for about 9 months.

Pepper and Pineapple Pickle

*With such a tongue-twisting title this pickle has to taste
delicious – and it does! It's tangy, spicy and quite mouth-watering
served with grilled gammon, bacon rolls or cold roast pork.*

Makes about 1.5–1.75 kg/3–4 lb

2 large green peppers
100 g/4 oz cooking apples
350 g/12 oz onions
225 g/8 oz demerara sugar
1 cinnamon stick
2 teaspoons mustard powder
2 tablespoons chopped fresh root ginger
1 large clove garlic, crushed
175 g/6 oz sultanas
1 (376-g/13¼-oz) can pineapple pieces
250 ml/8 fl oz red wine vinegar

Halve the peppers, remove the seeds and pith and roughly chop
the flesh. Peel, core and chop the cooking apples and chop the
onions. Mix the prepared ingredients in a large saucepan and
add the sugar, cinnamon, mustard, ginger and garlic. Stir in the
sultanas and the pineapple with its juice, then pour in the
vinegar.

Heat the mixture to boiling point, cover the pan and reduce
the heat. Cook the pickle at a steady simmer for 30 minutes,
stirring from time to time to make sure it does not stick to the
pan. Remove the lid from the pan and continue to cook for a
further 15 minutes.

Pour the pickle into warmed jars and cover these immediately
with airtight lids. Allow the pickle to mature for about 1
month; it can be stored for 6–9 months.

Beetroot and Orange Pickle

This is one of my favourite pickles and I often serve it as a side dish with simple meat grills. You don't have to wait for this preserve to mature – it will improve with keeping, but it is so good that it is usually eaten in great haste.

Makes about 1.5 kg/3 lb

1 kg/2 lb uncooked beetroot
450 g/1 lb onions
1 medium cooking apple
pared rind of 1 small orange
2 tablespoons finely chopped fresh root ginger
2 cloves garlic, crushed
300 ml/½ pint red wine vinegar
225 g/8 oz soft dark brown sugar

Peel the beetroot and dice it coarsely. Chop the onions and peel, core and slice the cooking apple. Chop the orange rind and mix it with all the prepared ingredients in a large saucepan. Add the ginger, garlic and vinegar and stir in the sugar.

Bring the pickle to the boil, cover the pan and reduce the heat, then allow it to simmer gently, stirring from time to time, for about 1½ hours. The beetroot should still be in chunks and the pickle should be quite juicy. Remove the lid and cook it for a further 20–30 minutes until the juices have thickened to coat the chunks of tender beetroot.

Transfer the pickle to warmed pots and cover these with airtight lids. It will be ready to eat at once and can be stored for about 6 months.

Courgette Pickle

(Illustrated on page 86)

This is an excellent way of using up large quantities of home-grown courgettes. Serve it with cold meat salads, cheese salads or as an accompaniment to plain pizzas and cheese fondues.

Makes about 1 kg/2 lb

450 g/1 lb courgettes
2 medium onions
225 g/8 oz cooking apples
2 large cloves garlic, crushed
300 ml/$\frac{1}{2}$ pint cider vinegar
175 g/6 oz sugar
100 g/4 oz sultanas

Peel the courgettes very thinly and dice them coarsely. Chop the onions and peel, core and slice the apples. Mix these prepared ingredients in a saucepan with the garlic, vinegar, sugar and sultanas and bring the mixture to the boil. Cover the pan, reduce the heat and simmer the pickle for 1 hour until thickened. Stir it from time to time to make sure it does not stick to the pan.

Pot the pickle into warmed jars and cover these immediately with airtight lids. Leave it to mature for 2 weeks. It can be stored for 6–9 months.

Aubergine Pickle

Warm and spicy, this pickle makes an excellent accompaniment to curries and spiced foods, so serve it with biriyanis and other rice dishes. It will also go equally successfully with grilled or barbecued meats and poultry and with simple fried or grilled fish.

Makes 1.75 kg/4 lb

1 kg/2 lb aubergines
salt
1 red pepper
2 medium onions
150 ml/¼ pint corn or sunflower oil
50 g/2 oz fresh root ginger, grated
3 cloves garlic, crushed
1 tablespoon garam masala
½ teaspoon chilli powder
75 g/3 oz sugar
300 ml/½ pint vinegar

Cut off and discard the stalks from the aubergines and cut the flesh into 2.5-cm/1-in cubes. Layer the cubes with a generous sprinkling of salt in a colander and leave them to stand for 1 hour.

Chop the pepper, removing the seeds and pith. Chop the onions and heat the oil in a saucepan. Add the onions to the pan followed by the ginger, garlic and pepper. Cook the mixture over a fairly low heat, stirring continuously, until the onion is soft but not browned. Add the spices and sugar to the pan and pour in the vinegar. Bring the mixture to the boil.

Shake the aubergine thoroughly in the colander to remove excess moisture and salt. Add the cubes to the boiling mixture and stir them in thoroughly. Return the pickle to the boil, reduce the heat, cover the pan and simmer it for about 15 minutes, stirring occasionally, until the vegetables are tender and the pickle has thickened.

Transfer it immediately to hot jars and cover these with airtight lids. Allow the pickle to mature for at least 2 weeks before eating it. It will keep for 6–9 months.

Mango Pickle

(Illustrated on page 103)

This is a mild, sweet and sour pickle – the sauce is sweet and the small pieces of cooked mango are quite tart. It is an excellent accompaniment with curries and also tastes delicious with cold roast pork or ham.

Makes about 1.5 kg/3 lb

2 green, unripe mangoes
350 g/12 oz cooking apples
450 g/1 lb onions
100 g/4 oz cooking dates
2 cloves garlic, crushed
350 g/12 oz light soft brown sugar
1 teaspoon ground ginger
300 ml/½ pint vinegar
salt and freshly ground black pepper

Peel the mangoes thinly and cut the flesh off the stones in large slices. Peel, core and slice the apples and chop the onions. Chop the dates and mix them in a large saucepan with the apples, onions, garlic, sugar, ginger and vinegar. Add a generous sprinkling of salt and pepper and bring the mixture to the boil, stirring to combine all the ingredients.

Reduce the heat and cover the pan, then simmer the pickle, stirring occasionally, for 20 minutes. Stir in the prepared mango and continue to cook, uncovered, for a further 40 minutes. The mixture should have thickened but the mango should still hold its shape.

Pot the pickle in warmed jars and cover these immediately with airtight lids. Mango pickle will taste best if it is allowed to mature for 2 weeks before being eaten and it can be stored for 6–9 months.

Gingered Pear Pickle

Pears, often plentiful and cheap in the shops, make a deliciously well-flavoured pickle to serve with meat salads, cold roast meats and pies and hot grills and barbecues. In fact you may well find that you serve this pickle with all your simple meals and snacks!

Makes about 1.5 kg/3 lb

1 kg/2 lb cooking pears
1 green pepper
2 large onions
100 g/4 oz cooking dates
2 tablespoons finely chopped root ginger
175 g/6 oz sugar
300 ml/$\frac{1}{2}$ pint vinegar
salt and freshly ground black pepper

Peel, core and slice the pears into a large saucepan. Remove the stalk, pith and seeds from the pepper and chop the flesh, together with the onions. Add them to the pan. Chop the dates and stir these in, followed by the ginger, sugar and vinegar. Add a generous sprinkling of salt and pepper and bring the pickle slowly to the boil.

Reduce the heat and simmer the pickle, uncovered, for about 1 hour or until the slices of pear are very soft and the preserve has thickened. Stir the mixture frequently during cooking to prevent it from sticking to the pan. Pot it in warmed jars and cover each immediately with an airtight lid. Allow the pickle to mature for 2–3 weeks; it can be kept for 6–9 months.

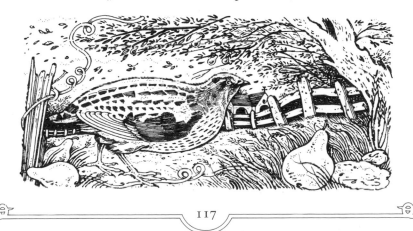

Brazil Nut and Apricot Pickle

(Illustrated on page 86)

I use whole brazil nuts in this tart pickle as they are sweet to the taste and provide an interesting contrast, both in texture and flavour, to the tangy dried apricots. If you prefer less obvious contrasts in food, chop the nuts before adding them to the mixture and increase the quantity of sugar by 50 g/2 oz.
Serve this pickle with cold roast turkey, roast or boiled meats and mild crumbly cheeses such as Cheshire and Caerphilly.

Makes 1 kg/2 lb

1 small onion
1 green chilli
2 stalks celery
225 g/8 oz dried apricots
350 g/12 oz shelled brazil nuts
75 g/3 oz sugar
300 ml/½ pint cider vinegar
grated rind and juice of 1 orange

Finely chop the onion and chilli. Chop the celery and apricots and mix them together with the onion and chilli in a saucepan. Add the nuts and sugar and pour in the vinegar. Finally, add the orange rind and juice and bring the mixture to the boil.

Cover the pan, reduce the heat and cook the pickle at a steady simmer, stirring occasionally, for 20–30 minutes. Transfer it to hot jars and cover these with airtight lids. This pickle will be ready to eat at once and will keep for 4–6 months.

NOTE For a stronger, spicy pickle, begin by placing the whole nuts in a bowl and sprinkle them with 25 g/1 oz salt, 1 teaspoon chilli powder and 50 g/2 oz grated fresh root ginger. Leave them to stand overnight before proceeding as above.

Walnut Pickle

This pickle is not cheap to prepare, but it is well worth the cost of the nuts as it is quite delicious both with cold roast meats and most varieties of cheese. Try a little with some ripe Brie or Camembert – the textures are very complementary.

Makes 1–1.4 kg/2–3 lb

1 onion
450 g/1 lb walnut pieces
4 tablespoons olive oil
2 teaspoons salt
$\frac{1}{2}$ teaspoon ground nutmeg
$\frac{1}{4}$ teaspoon paprika
75 g/3 oz dark soft brown sugar
2 cloves garlic
1 large cooking apple, peeled, cored and sliced
300 ml/$\frac{1}{2}$ pint vinegar

Finely chop the onion and chop any large walnut pieces. Heat the oil in a saucepan, add the onion and nuts and cook them over a low heat, stirring continuously, until the onion is soft but not browned. Add all the remaining ingredients and bring the pickle to the boil.

Cover the pan and simmer the mixture for 15–20 minutes. Stir it during cooking to prevent it from sticking to the pan. Transfer the pickle to hot jars, cover these with airtight lids and leave the pickle to mature for at least 2 weeks. It will keep for 4–6 months.

NOTE For a sweeter, spicier pickle increase the quantity of sugar to 225 g/8 oz and add 50 g/2 oz grated fresh root ginger.

Coconut Pickle

(Illustrated on page 103)

Fresh coconuts are now widely available in supermarkets and greengrocers and they make an excellent, well-flavoured, crunchy pickle. It is quite delicious with curries, spicy meat or fish dishes and mayonnaise-dressed salads.

Makes about 675 g/1½ lb

1 coconut
225 g/8 oz onions
3 cloves garlic, crushed
1 cinnamon stick
1 teaspoon salt
½ teaspoon ginger
generous pinch of chilli powder
300 ml/½ pint cider vinegar
50–100 g/2–4 oz sugar

Clean away the coarse outer hairs from the top of the coconut and pierce the three soft eyes with a meat skewer or corkscrew. Drain all the liquid out of the coconut into a large saucepan. Use a hammer to break the shell, then carefully cut all the flesh out of the inside. Grate the coconut on a coarse grater and mix it with the liquid in the pan.

Chop the onions and add them to the pan together with all the remaining ingredients, the exact amount of sugar depending on whether you like a sweet or a tart pickle. Do not add less sugar than the suggested minimum amount or the coconut will be too sharp.

Bring the mixture to the boil, stirring continuously to combine all the ingredients. Cover the pan, reduce the heat and allow the pickle to simmer for 30 minutes. Remove the lid from the pan and boil the pickle, stirring it occasionally to prevent it from sticking to the pan, for about 15 minutes, or until the juices have reduced and thickened.

Transfer the hot pickle to warmed pots and cover them immediately with airtight lids. This pickle is best if it is allowed to mature for a few weeks. It can be stored for 3–4 months.

Hot Lime Pickle

(Illustrated on page 103)

This is a recipe for devotees of curry! It is hot, spicy and oily and I was so pleased with the result when I first tried it that we had curry for dinner three nights running.

Makes a generous 450 g/1 lb

6 limes
2 tablespoons salt
2 teaspoons chilli powder
1 tablespoon garam masala
2 tablespoons sugar
6 cloves garlic, crushed
3 large onions
150 ml/$\frac{1}{4}$ pint oil
300 ml/$\frac{1}{2}$ pint vinegar

Roughly chop the limes and place them in a large basin. Mix the salt with the chilli powder, garam masala, sugar, and garlic. Sprinkle this mixture over the limes and toss them well in it to coat them thoroughly. Cover the basin and leave the limes to marinate for at least 24 hours – better still, leave them for three days.

Finely chop the onions. Heat the oil in a saucepan, add the onions and cook them until soft but not browned. Stir in the chopped limes with their juices and scrape all the spices out of the basin into the pan. Cook the mixture in the oil, stirring continuously, for 15 minutes. Pour in the vinegar and bring the pickle to the boil. Cover the pan and simmer it for 1 hour, stirring frequently to prevent the mixture from sticking to the bottom of the pan.

Transfer the pickle to warmed jars (a spoon is best for this), pressing the lime well down into the liquids. Cover each jar immediately with an airtight lid and allow the pickle to mature for 2 weeks. It can be stored for 6 months.

Beetroot Relish

(Illustrated on page 104)

Relishes, as their name suggests, are spicy and particularly suitable for serving with grills and barbecues.

Makes about 1.5 kg/3 lb

450 g/1 lb raw beetroot
450 g/1 lb cooking apples
350 g/12 oz onions
1 tablespoon finely chopped root ginger
2 large cloves garlic, crushed
1 teaspoon paprika
1 teaspoon turmeric
1 cinnamon stick
225 g/8 oz dark soft brown sugar
450 ml/$\frac{3}{4}$ pint vinegar

Peel the beetroot and apples and remove the core from the fruit, then grate both into a large saucepan. Finely chop the onions and add them to the pan together with all the remaining ingredients.

Bring the mixture to the boil, cover the pan, reduce the heat and simmer the relish, stirring occasionally, for about 1$\frac{1}{2}$ hours, until it has thickened and the beetroot is tender.

Transfer the relish to warmed jars and cover each with an airtight lid. Stand the preserve in a cool place for about 1 week to allow the flavour to mature. It will keep for 6–9 months.

Sweet Corn Relish

(Illustrated on page 104)

No selection of pickles and relishes would be complete without a recipe for the ever popular American corn relish. This is so good that I cheerfully eat it in the same quantities as I would a side salad! Traditionally served with hamburgers, it is also wonderful with pizzas, cottage pie, cold roast meats and cheese.

Makes about 1.5 kg/3 lb

2 large onions
1 green pepper
1 red pepper
4 sticks celery
4 tablespoons corn oil
1 teaspoon salt
1 large clove garlic, crushed
2 carrots
50 g/2 oz sugar
2 teaspoons mustard powder
675 g/1½ lb frozen sweet corn
450 ml/¾ pint vinegar

Chop the onions finely. Remove the stalks, seeds and pith from the green and red peppers and chop both finely. Similarly, finely chop the celery. Heat the oil in a large saucepan and add the chopped vegetables. Fry them until they are soft but not browned, then add the salt and garlic.

Cut the carrots into small cubes and add them to the pan together with all the remaining ingredients. Bring the mixture to the boil and cook it, uncovered, for 15 minutes. Stir the relish occasionally to prevent it from sticking to the pan.

Pot the relish in warmed jars, pressing the vegetables well down into the juices. Cover the jars immediately with airtight lids.

This relish does not need time to mature – it is juicy, tangy and crunchy and probably won't have time to mature before it is eaten! If not immediately consumed, however, it can be stored for 6 months.

Tomato and Onion Relish

(Illustrated on page 104)

*Here is a recipe which preserves the flavour of home-grown
tomatoes, with just some onions and a few spices to liven them up.
Serve this relish with grilled meats, sausages and barbecued
chicken – it is quite delicious.*

Makes 1.5–1.75 kg/3–4 lb

1 kg/2 lb ripe tomatoes
1 kg/2 lb onions
4 large cloves garlic, crushed
175 g/6 oz sugar
$\frac{1}{2}$ teaspoon turmeric
1 teaspoon paprika
300 ml/$\frac{1}{2}$ pint white vinegar

Place the tomatoes in a large bowl, cover them with boiling
water and allow them to stand for about 30 seconds. Drain, peel
and finely chop them. Finely chop the onions and mix them in a
large saucepan with the tomatoes and all the remaining
ingredients.

Bring the mixture to the boil, reduce the heat and cook it,
uncovered, for 1 hour. Stir the relish occasionally during
cooking to prevent it from sticking to the pan. Transfer it to
warmed pots, cover these immediately with airtight lids and
allow the relish to mature for at least 1 month. It can be stored
for 6–9 months.

Plum Relish

The idea for this relish comes from Chinese cooking. Plum sauce is one of the traditional accompaniments to Peking duck, but it can be difficult to obtain and plums are not always available if you want to prepare the sauce at home. Here is a recipe for a sweet, spicy preserve which is superb with roast duck or pork and also goes very well with cold meats and pork pie.

Makes about 1.75 kg/4 lb

2.25 kg/5 lb plums
350 g/12 oz cooking apples
450 g/1 lb onions
2 tablespoons chopped fresh root ginger
2 large cloves garlic, crushed
1 tablespoon mustard powder
1 teaspoon salt
1 cinnamon stick, broken
8 cloves
freshly ground black pepper
450 g/1 lb sugar
250 ml/8 fl oz vinegar

Halve the plums, remove the stones and roughly chop the flesh. Peel, core and roughly chop the apples and chop the onions. Place the plums, apples and onions together in a saucepan and add the ginger, garlic, mustard and salt. Tie the broken cinnamon stick with the cloves in a piece of muslin and place the bag in the pan. Season the mixture with a generous sprinkling of pepper, add the sugar and pour in the vinegar.

Bring the mixture to the boil, stirring frequently, lower the heat and partially cover the pan. Simmer the relish for $2-2\frac{1}{2}$ hours, until it is reduced to about half its original volume and has the consistency of a thick sauce. It is important to stir the mixture frequently during cooking to prevent it from sticking to the pan. Towards the end of the cooking time you may need to reduce the heat slightly to maintain a gentle simmering.

Remove the muslin-wrapped spices from the pan and pot the relish in warmed jars. Cover these immediately with airtight lids and leave the relish to mature for at least 2 weeks. It can be stored for 6–9 months.

Redcurrant Relish

(Illustrated on page 104)

Eaten in small quantities, here is a preserve which turns cold roast lamb into a feast. It will pep up a lamb grill or any barbecued meat.

Makes about 1 kg/2 lb

1 kg/2 lb redcurrants
1 kg/2 lb onions
4 cloves garlic, crushed
50 g/2 oz fresh root ginger
1 teaspoon turmeric
1 teaspoon salt
1 teaspoon ground cardamom
225 g/8 oz demerara sugar
300 ml/$\frac{1}{2}$ pint red wine vinegar

Top and tail the redcurrants. Finely chop the onions and place them in a large saucepan with the currants. Add the garlic. Grate the ginger and put it in the pan with the turmeric, salt, ground cardamom and sugar. Pour in the vinegar and bring the mixture to the boil. Reduce the heat until the relish is simmering rapidly, cover the pan and allow it to cook for about 1 hour.

Remember to stir the relish frequently during cooking so that it does not stick to the pan. At the end of the cooking time the fruit should be soft and pulpy and the juices thickened.

Transfer the relish to warmed pots and cover each immediately with an airtight lid. Allow it to mature for 2 weeks; it will keep for 6–9 months.

Index